Understanding
The Old Man and the Sea

The Greenwood Press "Literature in Context" Series
Student Casebooks to Issues, Sources, and Historical Documents

UNDERSTANDING
The Old Man and the Sea

A STUDENT CASEBOOK TO ISSUES, SOURCES, AND HISTORICAL DOCUMENTS

Patricia Dunlavy Valenti

The Greenwood Press
"Literature in Context" Series
Claudia Durst Johnson, Series Editor

GREENWOOD PRESS
Westport, Connecticut • London

Library of Congress Cataloging-in-Publication Data

Valenti, Patricia Dunlavy, 1945–
    Understanding The old man and the sea : a student casebook to issues, sources, and historical documents / Patricia Dunlavy Valenti.
        p. cm.—(The Greenwood Press "Literature in context" series ; ISSN 1074–598X)
    Includes bibliographical references and index.
    ISBN 0–313–31631–7 (alk. paper)
    1. Hemingway, Ernest, 1899–1961. Old man and the sea. 2. Hemingway, Ernest, 1899–1961. Old man and the sea—Sources. 3. Fishing stories, American—History and criticism. 4. Sea stories, American—History and criticism. 5. Aged men in literature. I. Title. II. Series.
    PS3515.E37 O5295   2002
    813'.52—dc21   2001055626

British Library Cataloguing in Publication Data is available.

Library of Congress Catalog Card Number: 2001055626
ISBN: 0–313–31631–7
ISSN: 1074–598X

First published in 2002

Greenwood Press, 88 Post Road West, Westport, CT 06881
An imprint of Greenwood Publishing Group, Inc.
www.greenwood.com

Printed in the United States of America

The paper used in this book complies with the Permanent Paper Standard issued by the National Information Standards Organization (Z39.48–1984).

10 9 8 7 6 5 4 3 2 1

Copyright Acknowledgments

Contents

Introduction

Shortly after *The Old Man and the Sea* had earned Ernest Hemingway the Nobel Prize for literature in 1954, he was interviewed by Robert Manning, who turned notes from that interview into an article for the *Atlantic Monthly* in 1965. Manning recounts the following incident, which had occurred while he was visiting Hemingway at Finca Vigía—the name of his villa in San Francisco de Paula, Cuba—nine years earlier:

> [Hemingway] reached for the mail, slit open one from a pile of fifteen letters. It was from a high school English teacher in Miami, Florida, who complained that her students rarely read good literature and relied for "knowledge" on the movies, television, and radio. To arouse their interest, she wrote, she told them about Hemingway's adventures and pressed them to read his writings. "Therefore, in a sense," she concluded, "you are the teacher in my tenth grade classroom. I thought you'd like to know it." Hemingway found that letter depressing: "Pretty bad if kids are spending all that time away from books." (Manning 107)

Little could Hemingway have guessed that by the beginning of the twenty-first century, books would have even more competitors for kids' attention. In addition to movies and television, video games, the Internet, myriad sports and club activities claim the time students might dedicate to reading works of fiction.

But teachers today still know exactly what that teacher who corresponded with Hemingway knew: Some students who won't read anything else will read works by Ernest Hemingway. Hemingway's life as a reporter and a war correspondent, as an ambulance driver in World War I, as a hunter and fisher of big game—in other words, his life as a blustering "real man"—appeals to even the most disaffected young person. Hemingway's no-nonsense style, devoid of apparent sentimentality, conveys narratives about war, love, death, and loss in a form acceptable even to adolescents typically discomforted by confronting these issues. Entering Hemingway's fictional universe, students have no fear that they will be embarrassed by an author who gives way to emotional display while exploring the courage and tenacity needed to endure life's strife and pain. Remarkably, even Hemingway's story about an old man who drifts at sea for three days in a failed attempt to catch a fish has appealed to adolescents for over five decades.

I first read this novella when I was a student in about seventh or eighth grade. Hemingway's language and the intensity of the situation he depicted stayed in my imagination with such clarity that when, several years ago, I read the novella again, I was amazed by my almost photographic recollection of lines and scenes. From my current vantage point and with the insights I have acquired through years as a college professor who teaches literature, supervises student teachers, and works with practicing teachers, I now see in *The Old Man and the Sea* opportunities for numerous lessons suiting a variety of learners. Teachers can tap the students' interests in history, geography, marine biology, sports, film, food—and, yes, literature—through a study of *The Old Man and the Sea*. Indeed, teachers may lure even the most recalcitrant students into reading the novella when his or her interest in baseball is captured.

When the Spencer Tracy film version of *The Old Man and the Sea* was released in 1958, it was promoted as an action-adventure movie. This publicity tactic obviously misrepresented the film as well as Hemingway's text, but readers of Hemingway's fiction do expect his plots to contain action, adventure, and romance. Those readers may be disappointed with the stillness of *The Old Man and the Sea*, a text that explores interior states and invisible victories. But *The Old Man and the Sea* is, nonetheless, a novella that can attract the very group of readers who are addicted to high-speed action in both life and film.

First of all, *The Old Man and the Sea* presents situations and emotions already known to many students (and their teachers). The novella represents a familiar family constellation. Many young people do not live in nuclear families; many live with grandparents and, like Manolin, experience their most important relationship with a much older adult, quite possibly an adult who is not related to them. *The Old Man and the Sea* allows such a student to enter into a world where this kind of relationship is valued and nurturing. Many young people believe that their efforts have not been, are not, and will not be requited by external reward or vindication. *The Old Man and the Sea* provides an arena to explore such feelings without preaching or formulaic answers.

Many high school students resent or reject the effort they must invest in reading classical literature, however worthwhile that effort is known to be. *The Old Man and the Sea* presents its narrative in uncomplicated, unadorned prose. Even the weakest reader should have no difficulty comprehending the literal meaning of this text, and without comprehension of literal meaning, as educators know, there can be no literary interpretation or progression to higher-order thinking skills. Thus this novella can be the first rung on the ladder of greater appreciation for other classical texts and works by other canonical writers.

Many of the students in today's classroom belong to "ethnic minorities"—a term that is meaningless in numerous school districts where the majority of students are not Caucasian. Indeed, Hispanics constitute the fastest-growing ethnic group in the United States today, and Hispanics are the majority population in many school settings. *The Old Man and the Sea* opens the dialogue about various Hispanic customs and the Spanish language. Many classrooms contain Cuban American students who can share their expertise about the culture implied by the novella's setting. Students from other Hispanic cultures can continue the exploration with information from their backgrounds. The student whose first language is Spanish will be the star of a lesson on this novella when she or he is asked to pronounce Spanish words, thereby demonstrating that second-language acquisition is of value to *all* students, not merely those who do not speak English. *The Old Man and the Sea* will thus become a step in fostering multilingual, multicultural knowledge.

Our exploration of *The Old Man and the Sea* and all of the issues raised above will allow the student of the work to access it from a variety of perspectives.

Chapter 1 examines the novella's formal elements of plot, setting character, point of view, and style. Additionally, this chapter situates Hemingway's work in the traditional literary genre to gain a fuller understanding of thematic nuances. Students will augment their skills in close reading and sensitivity to language and sentence structure. The "Topics for Written or Oral Exploration" section invites the student to engage in analyzing the novella by comparing it to other texts, including film and the text of their own lives.

Chapter 2 demonstrates that Hemingway embedded in the novella a full array of marine life proper to Cuba and its coastal waters. This chapter discusses numerous marine organisms well beyond the two most obviously associated with this work, the marlin and the shark. Teachers will be able to develop numerous multidisciplinary lessons using information from the interview inclded on marine organisms. And by more fully understanding the geography and climate of Cuba, students can assess the plausibility and realism of setting in the novella, characteristics of writing to which Hemingway always aspired.

Chapter 3 explores the historical factors that would have affected many facets of life for a man such as Santiago. His health, housing, and material resources were the result of a two-tier economic structure during the period before Fidel Castro's rule—the period of the novella's composition. This economic structure supported the few very rich (represented fleetingly by the tourists in the story) and the great masses of the very poor (represented by Santiago himself). Documents from contemporary travel magazines and from the writings of Castro, among others, demonstrate how different people viewed material circumstances in Cuba. For example, Santiago's palm hut, his *bohío*, is a picturesque element for one writer and a symbol of ignominious poverty for another.

Chapter 4 distinguishes the ethnic influence at play in the text. Cuba's African and Spanish heritages have yielded a culture wherein language, religion, gender attitudes, and food reflect racial and national origins. This chapter is calculated to give students an appreciation for cultural differences. At the same time, students are invited to interrogate the presentation of the "other" (Santiago) through the eyes of one from a different culture (Hemingway).

Chapter 5 examines not only baseball, but also the other sports mentioned in the novella. Allusions to baseball pervade the text, and although some of these references may be readily recognizable to today's audience, others were obscure even to the audience contemporary with the novella's publication. Newspaper and magazine reports illustrate the nature of baseball and its star players as they were viewed at the moment of the novella's composition. But baseball is not the only sport that informs this text. Arm wrestling and game fishing provide a context important to a valid thematic interpretation of *The Old Man and the Sea*. The ethos of the sportsman saturates this text. Without reflecting upon the documents that explain this ethos, we cannot understand the text.

Chapter 6 calculates how setting, plot, and character would have been affected by situating the novella in Castro's Cuba. Cuban economy as reflected in the tourist and commercial fishing industries, for example, would necessarily require a very different portrayal in Castro's Cuba. One quickly understands that the portrayal of activities that lack political consequence in Hemingway's text would become politically charged activities when played out within an evolving Communist nation.

I would like to conclude this introduction by acknowledging the help of many people. First of all, at the University of North Carolina at Pembroke, I am grateful to Jenny Bruns, my undergraduate research assistant during the summer of 2000; Robert Canida, Electronic Resources/Access Services librarian, for help with Interlibrary Loan Service; Cindy Saylor, Instructional Services/Reference librarian for help in locating copyright holders; Bonnie Kelley for assistance in preparing the chapter on the Cuban environment; Sarah-Lynn Brown for drawing the map of Cuba; Marie Oxendine for the illustration of marine organisms; Liliana Wendorff of the North Carolina Governor's Advisory Council on Hispanic/Latino Affairs for her thoughtful response to Chapter 4; Tina Emanuel, Computer Support Technician, for interview transcription; and the graduate students in EED552, "The Teaching of Literature," during the spring of 1999 and of 2001. These graduate students, who are practicing middle grade and high school teachers, opened my eyes to myriad possibilities for interdisciplinary study provided by any literary text. Among that group of graduate students, I particularly wish to thank Michael Roberts for his help with information pertaining to sports and Jan Gane, Ginger McMillan, Elizabeth Spangler, and Sandy Smith, whose comments on the novella helped to inform the preceding paragrah. I also wish to thank Karen Spach, a graduate student in diet and nutrition at the University of Wisconsin and members of the staff at the National Baseball Hall of Fame and the International Game Fishing Association for their cordial assistance in various aspects of my research.

I wish to thank my husband, Peter, for his help with the information on baseball for Chapter 5. Both he and my son, Marco, are ardent fans of the game, and I acknowledge here that whatever insight into baseball I may have communicated in this book derives from their appreciation of the sport.

Finally, I wish to pay special tribute to Dr. Arlyn Moeller, whose sudden death in December 2001 precludes his seeing his interview published in Chapter 3. Readers will glean from this "examination" of Santiago the compassion and insight that characterized Dr. Moeller's treatment of patients for over forty-five years. He will be sorely missed.

NOTE

Page references are to the Scribner edition of *The Old Man and the Sea*.

WORK CITED

Manning, Robert. "Hemingway in Cuba." *Atlantic Monthly* 216:2 (August 1965): 101–8.

1

A Literary Analysis of *The Old Man and the Sea*

In many ways, all that can be known of *The Old Man and the Sea* is revealed in its title. Possibly Ernest Hemingway's most enduring work of fiction, *The Old Man and the Sea* is a very simple, brief story of an old man, a Cuban fisherman named Santiago, whose life differs greatly from the lives of the young Americans who read about him today. Santiago is a poor, solitary man whose possessions consist of little more than the clothes he wears. But Santiago is rich in determination and perseverance, and he refuses to succumb to a streak of bad luck. When the novella opens, he has gone eighty-four days without catching a fish—without, in other words, success in making a living as a fisherman. On the eighty-fifth day, Santiago sets out to sea again—alone—and, after an enormous struggle, he catches the biggest marlin he has ever seen or imagined, only to have it destroyed by sharks. At the end of the story, Santiago's material situation is no different than it was at the beginning. He is alone in his shack without having brought to shore a fish to sell at market.

If readers judge Santiago only in terms of his material success, then he is indeed a failure in a pointless story. But Hemingway prevents readers from accepting that position by taking them through every moment of Santiago's three days and nights at sea and forcing them to assess the worth of Santiago's actions and the eventual outcome of his efforts by other than exclusively material standards. Readers come to respect Santiago for his indomitable will, self-discipline, and focus. These characteristics cause readers to question with Santiago the meaning of both his achievement and his loss.

EXPOSITION OF ELEMENTS OF FICTION

Longer and more complex than a short story but shorter and more compact than a novel, *The Old Man and the Sea* can be classified as a *novella* or *novelette*, a work of fiction typically fifty to one hundred pages long. As such, *The Old Man and the Sea* lacks the chapter divisions that organize events in a novel. The story's events can, however, be divided according to points in time. *The Old Man and the Sea* begins on land, and five days later it ends on land. Examining the narration of the first day and night on land, the reader obtains those facts needed to understand what will come. This is where the *exposition*—the presentation of the introductory material of a work of fiction—occurs and where the reader is grounded in the novella's characters, setting, conflict, and tone. With an understanding of these elements of fiction, the reader can begin to interpret the novella's *theme*—that dominant, abstract idea made concrete and comprehensible through all the elements of plot, setting, character, and point of view.

Plot can be defined as that sequence of events that reveals the basic conflict of the narrative, whether that conflict be between the person and self, society, or environment. *Setting* refers to where and when the narrative takes place. Specific place or places, geographical location, environmental characteristics, and daily manner of living, as well as the particular time or period of history in which the narrative occurs, all constitute aspects of its setting. The element of *character* is created in a number of ways—by what characters say, by what characters say about other characters, by what characters do, and by what the narrator reveals about the characters. *Point of view* determines the manner by which the reader is presented the materials of the story. The narrator may be an omniscient third person outside the story who possesses all knowledge of the characters—their thoughts and actions—and all knowledge of events, whether they be past, present, or future; the omniscient narrator may also limit this knowledge to the revelation of a particular character's perspective. Another way authors deliver a narrative is through the first-person narrator who is also a character in the story and who must necessarily limit the presentation of the story to what is plausible knowledge for that character.

Although much of the exposition in *The Old Man and the Sea* is presented through *dialogue*, or conversation, between the two main characters—Santiago, the old man, and Manolin, the young boy—the bulk of the story is presented through a third-person narrator. This technique limits the unfolding of events to the workings of Santiago's unconscious and conscious mind. Santiago's unconscious is rendered through the presentation of his dreams. Santiago's conscious thoughts are presented through the limited omniscient narrator. In *The Old Man and the Sea*, however, this narrative point of view often employs a *stream of consciousness* technique, which presents the random and associative quality of a character's conscious thoughts. For example, while at sea, Santiago realizes that his thoughts hop from his quest for marlin to his recollection of an arm wrestling match or Joe DiMaggio's bone spurs. Frequently, these thoughts—sometimes spoken aloud to himself or formed as mental conversation—are signaled by the use of direct quotation, but just as often Hemingway makes the transition between the narrator and the protagonist without the benefit of quotation marks. For instance, immediately after the marlin takes Santiago's bait, Hemingway writes: "This far out, he [the marlin] must be huge this month, he [Santiago] thought. Eat them, fish. Eat them. Please eat them" (41). The first sentence renders Santiago's thought indirectly, but the second, third, and fourth sentences present what amounts to direct quotation of Santiago's thoughts about the marlin taking the bait without the conventional signal of quotation marks. This technique, used repeatedly throughout the novella, forges a seamless transition between the narrator's third-person omniscient point of view and Santiago's words and thoughts. Thus, although the plot of this novella suggests a high level of action—even adventure—the actual drama in *The Old Man and the Sea* occurs in Santiago's mind as he analyzes the tasks before him, recalls past situations, and contemplates the meaning of events.

Santiago is introduced as an impoverished old fisherman. His skin is furrowed and weathered by exposure to the elements, and his body, though very thin, reveals traces of its former prowess.

He lives alone in a shack made of palm, where he sleeps on bedding composed of box springs covered with newspaper; his pillow consists of his pants, worn daily and rolled up with great care each night to cushion his head. Worse than Santiago's poverty is his apparent bad luck as a fisherman, which makes him the subject of ridicule among some villagers. Nonetheless, Santiago retains the admiration and affection of Manolin. The boy continues to regard Santiago with respect, for Manolin has learned much about fishing from the old man, and Manolin's concern about the aging fisherman is apparent in the boy's efforts to bolster Santiago's confidence and to ensure that he has nourishment. In this way, the expected roles played by a boy and an old man are immediately reversed, with the youth caring for the needs of the adult. Rather than regarding Santiago as a burden, Manolin reveres the old man for his past accomplishments and hopes that Santiago will once again demonstrate his skill as a great fisherman. Hence Manolin offers to fish with Santiago, but the old man refuses the offer in his solicitude for the young boy, who may himself be judged unlucky by association with Santiago.

During the exposition of narrative facts, Hemingway creates the setting for the novella, a fishing village that reflects the poverty of the working class in Cuba during the decades preceding the composition of *The Old Man and the Sea*. To further create the Cuban ambience, Hemingway laces Santiago's and Manolin's dialogue with Spanish words and grammatical constructions. The discussion of baseball provides another interesting element of exposition. Both the boy and the old man have detailed knowledge of the American baseball players and teams. The Yankees are their favorite team, and they particularly admire Joe DiMaggio. Santiago feels a special identification with DiMaggio, recalling that the baseball player's father was a poor fisherman and assuming, therefore, that DiMaggio would understand the life of fishermen. Santiago hopes that one day he might take DiMaggio fishing. Such thoughts of the future are balanced by thoughts of the past as Santiago reminisces about his youthful work as a seaman, which brought him to Africa. When he sleeps, he dreams of lions roaming the African beach, just as he had seen them there many years ago. Both Santiago's dreaming of the lions and his waking thoughts of DiMaggio will become recurring elements throughout the novella.

At the point in the novella when Santiago leaves shore, the exposition phase of the narrative concludes, for the reader possesses the essential facts: The story will take place in Cuba or off its shores; and the narrative will unfold with Santiago as the point-of-view character and with Manolin as the other main character, but one of lesser importance. The basic plot of the novella will involve Santiago's attempts to catch a fish, maintain his livelihood, and recapture his reputation as a master fisherman, but the *conflict*—the overarching challenge the central character of a story must face—promises to be more complex than that of a man confronting nature. Manolin's early question to Santiago about whether the old man is still physically capable of bringing in a big fish provides an element of *foreshadowing*, the suggestion of events to come. Is the sea Santiago's only opponent, or is his creeping debility, old age, or bad luck his real adversary? Thus Hemingway carefully and subtly establishes his *tone*, the emotional attitude that the author takes toward his subject and, consequently, the emotional attitude the reader adopts. We do not pity Santiago in his poverty and solitude; rather, we share Manolin's respect for the old man, who will not give up in the face of adversity.

PLOT

From the moment Santiago departs from land, the events of *The Old Man and the Sea* can be divided into the old man's three days and nights at sea and the morning of his return to shore. During his first day at sea, the reader observes Santiago's very deliberate method of fishing, and the reader obtains a clear picture of the birds that fly about, as well as the fish and their habits. Early in the day, Santiago catches a ten-pound albacore tuna, which he uses for bait, but it is the strike of the enormous marlin that is the day's significant event, the one that suggests that Santiago's luck has turned. As this day concludes, Santiago ignores his discomfort and hunger; instead, he focuses his effort upon keeping the marlin hooked, thinking briefly about baseball and wishing occasionally that Manolin had accompanied him. "I wish I had the boy" (45), says Santiago in his first use of what amounts to a quasi *refrain*, a group of words or phrases repeated at intervals, a device more typically used in poetry. The old man's words about the boy will recur during his first night at sea and several other times in the novella when Santiago reflects upon his remote, isolated situation.

During Santiago's second day at sea, his condition is debilitated by a lack of sleep and proper nourishment. He converses aloud with the birds and with the fish that he has hooked; he even talks to himself. His hands become a factor in the narrative now—the right one bleeding, the left one cramping. Talking about his hands and appetite as if they were things separate from him, Santiago forces himself to eat some of the raw tuna. He is sustained by this unpalatable food, by the recollection of a long-past victory in an arm wrestling competition, and by his thoughts of DiMaggio, who had overcome injury in order to continue playing baseball. When the fish breaks water, Santiago realizes that it is the biggest marlin he has ever seen, and the old man patiently awaits precisely the right moment to spear the fish, even as he realizes that sharks may come. Santiago spends his second night at sea trying not to fall asleep and convincing himself that his pain is not important but that the endurance to fulfill his quest is.

As the sun rises on a third day at sea, Santiago is aware that his struggle is similar to the marlin's: Both are attempting to survive. At last Santiago triumphs and, through an enormous effort, kills the marlin. Fastening it to the side of his small boat, Santiago begins to row toward shore. Killing the marlin constitutes the *climax* of the narrative, that turning point or moment when rising action ceases and falling action begins. Just when it seems that Santiago's achievement exceeds anything he could have imagined, a mako shark attacks the marlin. Though this first shark attack is introduced abruptly into the narrative, it had been foreshadowed subtly much earlier with Santiago's brief worry about sharks. Santiago succeeds in fending off the mako shark only to have two *galano* (shovelnose) sharks attack. Although it becomes apparent that Santiago's efforts are futile, he continues to fight off the marlin's predators while he questions the reasons for this loss. Night falls and Santiago, at the point of exhaustion, notices that his boat moves toward shore more swiftly with its gigantic fish reduced to a carcass.

Santiago arrives at port under cover of darkness, early in the fifth day of the narrative. He secures his small boat and carries its mast back to his shack, where he falls deeply asleep. Manolin discovers him at daylight and attempts to minister to the old man. Crying, Manolin goes for coffee while tourists inquire with confusion and curiosity about the carcass of the great marlin. Thus the *denouement*, or the resolution of all elements of the plot, occurs.

CHARACTER

Manolin

Critics of *The Old Man and the Sea* have puzzled over Manolin's age. Some think of him as a teenager, although one critic believes him to be no more than ten years old. Throughout the text, both the narrator and Santiago refer to Manolin as "the boy." But Manolin's knowledge of fishing, his physical strength, and his mature desire to provide for Santiago's needs while preserving the old man's dignity seem more the traits of a young man than a child. Perhaps more important than fixing Manolin's age with certainty, then, is understanding the relationship that exists between him and Santiago, for in some ways, Manolin functions as a *foil* to Santiago, a character whose purpose in a work of fiction is to clarify the reader's understanding and appreciation of the principal character.

Manolin's relationship to Santiago is that of an "apprentice" or a "disciple," each word connoting slightly different functions. As Santiago's apprentice, Manolin has learned how to be a fisherman; consequently, he is indebted to the old man for his skill and his livelihood. As Santiago's disciple, Manolin has acquired values such as diligence and patience and thereby fashions his behavior upon the example set by the old man. Thus Santiago functions as Manolin's mentor. Providing the boy with more than merely a way to make his living, Santiago demonstrates for Manolin what values are important in a man's life.

Although Manolin is clearly indebted to Santiago, the *viejo* (old man) owes his own debt to the boy, for the old man's image of himself depends in part upon being viewed as a worthy master. That the boy's parents now prohibit Manolin from fishing with Santiago must be a devastating blow to his ego. Although the boy does not embark on this fishing trip with Santiago, the old man later wishes numerous times that the boy were with him at sea because Santiago increasingly recognizes the limitations imposed by his age, his infirmities, and his solitude. Like his frequent think-

Gregorio Fuentes and an unnamed young man in a skiff. Photograph by Mary Hemingway/ Hemingway Collection, John F. Kennedy Library, Boston.

ing about Joe DiMaggio, invoking thoughts of the absent boy fortifies Santiago for his arduous task by motivating him to remain a worthy master. In an important way, Manolin's and Santiago's roles have been reversed, for it is Manolin who inspires Santiago's strength.

The nature of this relation can be clarified by contrasting it with a similar relationship in another great American novella that centers on a quest in the natural world. William Faulkner's *The Bear* was published in 1942, just ten years before *The Old Man and the Sea*. In this story, young Ike McCaslin participates in his family's annual attempt to kill the fierce bear Old Ben. Instructed in the skill and wisdom of the hunt by the men of his family and by Sam Fathers, Ike is the one—not his tutors—who must prove himself. Killing the bear becomes Ike's ritual initiation into the meaning of his place in his family and the world his family inhabits. In *The Old Man and the Sea*, killing the fish represents the old man's attempt to hold on to a place in his society, which is slipping away from him, bereft as he is of family, luck, and, perhaps, skill.

Santiago

The solitary life of this character engenders both the reader's sympathy and admiration. Santiago has removed a picture of his wife from the wall in his shack; it is too poignant a reminder of his lack of close relationships or relatives. With deliberate, almost ritualized actions, Santiago exhibits great dignity in caring for his few possessions and securing his fishing equipment from the remote possibility of theft. He refuses to borrow from other village folk, and Manolin respects Santiago's efforts to sustain the impression that his poverty is not so extreme that he has had to sell his cast net. Santiago's rejection of Manolin's offer to fish with him indicates the old man's independence as much as it demonstrates his generosity.

During his three days at sea, Santiago exhibits even greater fortitude in his solitary quest. Relying entirely on his own resources to catch the great marlin, he endures extreme fatigue, hunger, and exposure to the elements. Not having brought a provision of food with him, Santiago catches, kills, and eats some raw tuna and shrimp, taking care to eat slowly and thus avoid nausea. He rations what little water he has brought on his boat, and he leans against the fishing line, using the weight of his own body to keep the marlin hooked during the long effort needed to reel it to the side of the boat for the kill.

Santiago relies upon no one and nothing but himself to control the discomfort and pain that occur during his lonely ordeal. When his hand cramps, he talks to it as if it is a thing apart from himself, telling it that the warmth of the sun will eventually release the cramp. So focused is Santiago on his task that he does not immediately realize when his other hand begins to bleed from a cut caused by the line. Santiago regards these problems with his hands as his body's betrayal, implying that his body is an entity distinct from himself.

Rather than be defeated by these enemies of physical pain and loneliness, Santiago focuses his mind in ways calculated to bolster his resolution and confidence. He deliberately recalls the former strength of his hands, proven in the arm wrestling match he had won against an opponent who was reported to be the strongest man in the area. Santiago also brings to mind Joe DiMaggio, who, despite adversity, prevailed as a legendary baseball player. This realization inspires Santiago as he might have been inspired by a heroic event in the life of a saint, for Santiago thinks, "I must be worthy of the great DiMaggio who does all things perfectly even with the pain of the bone spur in his heel" (68).

While the reader admires Santiago for his independence, courage, and tenacity, the degree to which Santiago practices these virtues may also cause the reader to question whether these characteristics remain positive traits. Santiago's assertion that "pain does not matter to a man" (84) bespeaks "machismo," originally a Spanish word that has come into the English language to signify the extreme display of such manly characteristics as independence, toughness, courage, and physical prowess. Clearly, Santiago admires and emulates DiMaggio because he possesses those macho, or manly, qualities.

Santiago's belief in the value of his own independence is challenged, however, by the events of this three-day quest. Venturing out so far alone, Santiago must recognize that Manolin would have been useful to him. Santiago realizes that he has neglected several preparations that might have made his effort more successful. He ought to have secured a larger supply of freshwater, and he should have brought some salt with which to cure the raw fish he is forced to eat. Although Santiago is entirely at home at sea, capable as he is of smelling the direction of the wind and conversing with the fish and birds as brothers, he recognizes that he is bereft of other human beings. Santiago knows that at his age, being alone, even though it affirms his independence, is not a good thing. And the courage he displayed in venturing so far out into the ocean may be seen as a kind of *hubris*, a term that defines the excessive pride, confidence, and ambition that lead to the downfall of a tragic hero. Santiago's boast to the marlin, "I will show him what a man can do" (64), can be read as an ironic commentary on the final outcome of Santiago's struggle. Perhaps a man cannot do what he attempts.

Hemingway has created in Santiago a character whose actions are governed by carefully directed thoughts. He controls all facets of his conscious life with great care. His actions—whether these be folding his pants or baiting a hook—are so deliberate that they take on the significance of a "ritual," a prescribed ceremony that elevates mundane behavior to a quasi-sacred level. Santiago responds to bodily sensations of pain or fatigue with the control of a person who lives by the slogan "Mind over matter." For that reason, he is particularly affronted by the cramp in his hand, a conspicuous reminder that mere willpower cannot control his body. And turning his thoughts to positive inspirations such as his championship arm wrestling match or to Joe DiMaggio demonstrates his persistent, conscious control over his mental processes.

The deliberateness of Santiago's thoughts and actions contrasts with another important recurring element in the novella, Santiago's dreams. Several times during the novella, Santiago sleeps and has recurring dreams, one of which is about a pride of lions playing on an African shore, a sight he had seen as a young man. The last words of the novella are spoken by the narrator who says, "The old man was dreaming about the lions" (127). Although the lions constitute dream images whose source lies in Santiago's own past, the dream lion provides a *symbol*, an object with an abstract meaning beyond the physical image. Lions are undisputed symbols of strength and ferocity; the lion is, after all, commonly called "the king of beasts."

But beyond providing symbolic associations, Hemingway's inclusion of Santiago's dream life introduces the element of the old man's unconscious mind, which contrasts markedly with the great emphasis placed upon Santiago's conscious thought throughout the novella. Although Santiago's recurring dream about the lions brings him back to his youth and to the time of his physical strength, this dream takes him away from the ordinary concerns of adult life. Early in the novella, the narrator informs us that Santiago no longer dreams about physical competitions or romantic relationships or tremendous catches of fish. In his dreams, Santiago escapes the need to struggle and endure. He has let go of—given up control over—his livelihood, his relationships, and his aspirations to be a champion. His dreams suggest that the old man may be ready for death, for Santiago no longer has an appetite. He eats without pleasure, only—reluctantly—to sustain himself.

THEME

How should the reader interpret the meaning of *The Old Man and the Sea*? The answer to this question will reside to a large degree in the values that the reader holds. Like Santiago, the reader may believe that "A man can be destroyed but not defeated" (103), that the human demonstration of endurance is a triumph in its own right. The magnitude of Santiago's effort is such that, for many readers, it represents the epitome of the human spirit. "Grace under pressure" is a phrase that was coined to describe the typical Hemingway protagonist's ability to endure enormous pain and loss without dissolving into sentimentality or self-pity. Without a doubt, Santiago demonstrates the "grace under pressure" of the Hemingway "code hero," a man who tenaciously adheres to the rules of whatever game he may be playing, notwithstanding his apparent defeat.

Another interpretation of *The Old Man and the Sea* lies in the regret that Santiago expresses with the words, "I am sorry that I went too far out. I ruined us both" (115). Perhaps Santiago's confidence in his own capacity is a form of pride that actually causes the loss of his livelihood and the pointless destruction of the marvelous fish. This interpretation suggests a reading of *The Old Man and the Sea* as a classical tragedy in which the hero's downfall is the consequence of his character flaw. A more contemporary, feminist reading of this novella would also support a thematic interpretation of the conclusion as an indictment of Santiago's pride, specifically his pride in a macho ethos that brings about its own destruction and failure.

Viewing the theme of *The Old Man and the Sea* more broadly than as a commentary on an individual's life, we may examine what this novella tells us about human interaction with the natural world. Hemingway vehemently denied that *The Old Man and the Sea* exemplified *naturalism*, a term often applied to the work of many of Hemingway's late-nineteenth- and early-twentieth-century literary predecessors, including Stephen Crane, Theodore Dreiser, and Frank Norris, among others. Naturalism suggests not merely a literary technique—the scientific presentation of the natural world—but a philosophical attitude. The world of the naturalist is one of determinism and pessimism; humans cannot freely choose their destinies but are manipulated by forces larger than any individual choice or action. Notwithstanding Hemingway's assertions to the contrary, the events in *The Old Man and the Sea* might seem, at least on the surface, to fit the definition of naturalism. Nothing Santiago does or decides affects the outcome of the narrative, which appears to be determined by forces entirely outside his control. A more contemporary interpretation of the ways in which *The Old Man and the Sea* comments upon humans and the natural environment might take the ecological approach suggested by Santiago's own words, "Man is not much beside the great birds and beasts" (68). While the novella reveals that Santiago respects his kinship with other living beings in the natural world, we may also judge Santiago's killing of the marlin as evidence of the arrogance with which humans seek to dominate, rather than coexist with, nature.

Yet another theme is suggested by Santiago's question "Luck is a thing that comes in many forms and who can recognize her?" (117). Perhaps life's events are ultimately inscrutable, for Santiago's situation is a paradox. He is, simultaneously, a most fortunate man to have caught the biggest marlin ever imagined and a most unfortunate man to have gone to sea eighty-five times without bringing home a catch.

Some critics have sought to understand *The Old Man and the Sea* by seeing symbolic values in several of Santiago's actions that resemble those of the Christ figure. Santiago's bleeding hand, reminiscent of stigmata, is recalled in an *allusion*—the reference to a literary or historical event—made by the narrator, who compares Santiago's cry of pain to the sound a man would make upon having his hand nailed to a piece of wood. Santiago's three-day ordeal at sea and his climb up a hill with the mast of his boat across his shoulders suggest similarities to Christ's three-day entombment and his carrying the cross to Calvary. These allusions to Christ could support a thematic interpretation that suggests that Santiago's suffering has redemptive value, if only the redemption of his own self-image.

Yet another interpretation of *The Old Man and the Sea* sees in the novella a reflection of Hemingway's own life. In fact, a biographical interpretation of *The Old Man and the Sea* appeared in an editorial in the September 1952 edition of *Life* magazine, which contained the novella's initial publication. Readers then and now may compare the character of Santiago with Hemingway himself. Santiago is a perfectionist about all details of fishing; Hemingway crafted his writing with immense care. Santiago has endured a lengthy spell during which he could catch no fish; Hemingway had gone a decade without publishing a highly acclaimed novel. Santiago is no longer regarded by the villagers as an undisputed master fisherman; Hemingway's reputation as a master of his craft had been questioned by some critics. Santiago struggles with the effects of aging on his professional abilities; Hemingway had recently turned fifty and had begun to question whether he was past his prime. Santiago is alone; his wife is dead. Hemingway had experienced the death of several people close to him. His mother, Grace Hemingway; his former wife and the mother of his children, Pauline Phieffer Hemingway; and his publisher, Charles Scribner, all died during the year that Hemingway was writing *The Old Man and the Sea*. A final comparison between Santiago and Hemingway lies in the fact that they both face "sharks." For Hemingway, these would be the critics, who, with their bad reviews, could destroy his achievement.

Hemingway's own words encourage these comparisons. In his remarks to the Swedish Academy upon receipt of the Nobel Prize, Hemingway wrote:

> Writing, at its best, is a lonely life. . . . [The writer] does his work alone and if he is a good enough writer he must face eternity, or the lack of it, each day. . . . He should try for something that has

never been done or that others have tried and failed. Then sometimes, with great luck, he will succeed. . . . It is because we have
had such great writers in the past that a writer is driven far out past
where he can go, out to where no one can help him. (Quoted in
Baker 528–29)

These words might easily be Hemingway's description of Santiago.
Alone and beyond the help of others, with both skill and luck, he
may succeed where others have not.

But Hemingway was quick to disavow biographical or any other
kind of symbolic interpretation. He told a critic, as Carlos Baker
recounts the conversation, that "Sea equaled sea, old man was old
man, the boy was a boy, the marlin was itself, and the sharks were
no better and no worse than other sharks" (Baker 505). Another
writer, Robert Manning, who profiled Hemingway in Cuba after
the publication of *The Old Man and the Sea*, makes the following
point about symbolism in the novella: Hemingway, says Manning,
"had tried to make everything in the story real—the boy, the sea,
and the marlin and the sharks, the hope being that each would
mean many things. In that way, the parts of the story become symbols, but they are not first designed or planted as symbols" (104).

GENRE

The Old Man and the Sea is a work of fiction, but what kind of
a work of fiction is it? Any work of literature may be grouped according to its form or technique, and these groupings or classifi-
cations of literature are called *genres*. We may better understand
the power of such a simple story by placing it in the context of the
great literary genres.

Some critics have classified *The Old Man and the Sea* with such
works of literature as the fable, parable, and allegory, works whose
avowed purpose is to teach a lesson about human experience. A
fable is a short narrative that frequently employs animals as characters. Written in either poetry or prose, a fable communicates a
truth or a caution about virtue and vice. Some of the earliest fables
are attributed to the author known as Aesop, who is said to have
lived in Greece during the sixth century before the Christian era.
In seventeenth-century France, Jean de La Fontaine wrote some of
the fables we still know today, such as "The Hare and the Tortoise"

and "The Fox and the Grapes." In nineteenth- and early-twentieth-century American literature, Joel Chandler Harris's *Uncle Remus and Brer Rabbit* contains examples of fables. Immediately after publication of *The Old Man and the Sea*, Mark Schorer said in his review that the novella was like a fable because of its simple recounting of generalizations about human life.

A *parable* is similar to a fable in its use of storytelling for a moral purpose, but the circumstances of the parable are more realistic and the characters are human. For example, the biblical story about "The Pearl of Great Price" is a parable that teaches that eternal life is worth whatever the price one must pay for it. In this parable, a man discovers an extremely valuable pearl, and he sells all his possessions so that he may have the money to buy that pearl. The reader may see similarities between this parable and Santiago's single-minded quest for the marlin.

Both the fable and the parable share characteristics with the *allegory*, a kind of fiction in which every element in the story stands for something outside of the narrative itself. In an allegory, setting, plot, and character each represent or symbolize values that transcend the actual story. John Bunyan's *Pilgrim's Progress* is a renowned allegory written in seventeenth-century England about the hero. Christian's effort to triumph over worldly evils named Vanity Fair, the Slough of Despond, and Mr. Worldly Wiseman. An allegory is intended to express a truth about human life, and some critics consider *The Old Man and the Sea* to be an allegory that tells us something about the extent and limits of human capabilities; others, as pointed out above, see the novella as an allegory of Hemingway's own life.

Still others liken *The Old Man and the Sea* to an epic. An *epic* is usually a long, narrative poem that recounts the deeds of a hero whose extraordinary, even superhuman accomplishments are of great significance to a race or a nation. Homer's *The Odyssey* is an example of an ancient Greek epic in which the hero, Odysseus, returns home after the Trojan War. Obviously, *The Old Man and the Sea* is not a long poem, nor do the events recounted in it have racial or national significance. Santiago does, however, perform extraordinary feats, but because the story does not have the proportions and scope of an epic, some may think it has more in common with the tall tale.

The *tall tale* is a genre that originated on the American frontier.

Anecdotes surrounding such folk heroes as Davy Crockett, Paul Bunyan, and John Henry are good examples of tall tales. Characterized by the exaggerated narration of impossible happenings that are described with realistic detail, the tall tale is typically told for humorous effect. Although many critics charge Hemingway with exaggerating Santiago's accomplishment beyond the limits of realism, the element of humor is conspicuously lacking in *The Old Man and the Sea*.

STYLE

For half a century, readers have enjoyed *The Old Man and the Sea*. What many readers recall years after they have read the novella is Hemingway's deliberate description of Santiago's actions and surroundings. It is worthwhile to examine how a writer's style produces this kind of memorable clarity.

Undoubtedly, Hemingway's experience as a reporter affected his style. His sentences are uncomplicated in their direct conveying of information. Notice how the following sentence presents the facts of Santiago's situation, linking the subject to verbs with the simple conjunction "and": "He knelt down and found the tuna under the stern with the gaff and drew it toward him keeping it clear of the coiled lines" (57). At no time does the narrator intrude with any indication of what the reader should think or feel about the events described, and the narrator maintains this objectivity even when events are far more momentous than the routine handling of a fish.

Consider, now, Hemingway's narration of very dramatic events. After the old man has caught the huge marlin and lashed the fish to his boat, we have a paragraph describing Santiago's activities. He soaks his hands; he observes the clouds. Hemingway concludes this paragraph thus: "The old man looked at the fish constantly to make sure it was true. It was an hour before the first shark hit" (99–100). The shark attack is a decisive moment in the novella, the moment when both the reader and Santiago can no longer hope that his efforts will bring success. But the shark attack is introduced without emotional fanfare, commentary, or judgment. A person reading too quickly might miss the importance of what has occurred.

In an interview published in the *Paris Review* in 1958, Hemingway said about his craft: "I always try to write on the principle of the iceberg" (Plimpton 84). Hemingway's "iceberg theory" of prose style suggests that the writer should leave unsaid the vast majority of what might be written on a subject. The reader, presented with only the tip of the iceberg, is left to infer the magnitude of events and emotions beneath the surface. Hemingway was a master at leaving unseen and unsaid what another writer might have overstated. Specifically talking about *The Old Man and the Sea*, Hemingway cited information about the sea, fishing, and fishermen that he chose to omit from the story. Knowing what to leave out gives a writer power, just as the force of an iceberg is created by that seven-eighths of its bulk that is never seen.

In addition to understanding how Hemingway achieves this clarity and economy of style, we may also understand why this particular style fits the theme of *The Old Man and the Sea*. This simple, unadorned style suits the story of a simple man in unadorned surroundings, a man who exemplifies the "grace under pressure" of Hemingway's protagonists and their almost stoical struggle against overwhelming odds. Although Santiago's enormous effort does not result in success, he does not waste words in overly emotional self-pity or excessive rationalization. This quiet acceptance, further evidence of "grace under pressure," is aptly expressed through Hemingway's sparse style.

TOPICS FOR WRITTEN OR ORAL EXPLORATION

Topics Focusing on the Text

1. Consider how *The Old Man and the Sea* would have been a different story if (a) Santiago had taken Manolin with him or (b) if Santiago had caught an average-sized fish. Remaining faithful to other elements of characterization and setting, describe in as much detail as possible a plot that includes either of these circumstances. Determine how the difference in plot would affect both the denouement of the story and possible thematic interpretations.

2. Santiago recalls past events in his life. List all of the remembered events and determine the narrative function of these—contrasted with the memories Santiago might have recalled—during this five-day period of the novella.

3. Santiago's situation at the end of *The Old Man and the Sea* seems to be exactly the same as it was at the beginning of the novella. Write an essay in which you argue that Santiago is either a *static* character (one to whom things happen but without those events causing any internal realizations) or a *dynamic* character (one who is changed somehow by the events that he experiences).

4. Toward the end of the novella, Santiago says:

   • "A man can be destroyed but not defeated."

   • "I am sorry that I went out too far. I ruined us both."

   • "Luck is a thing that comes in many forms and who can recognize her?"

   • "Man is not much beside the great birds and beasts."

   Select the statement that most closely articulates your judgment about the theme of the novella. Using additional evidence from the text, write an essay in which you argue why your chosen statement represents the theme of *The Old Man and the Sea*.

5. Write an essay in which you compare and contrast the two portions of the novella set on land. By analyzing the people and their words and actions in these two episodes, determine how the conclusion of the novella differs from its exposition. Do these differences tell you anything about the theme of *The Old Man and the Sea*?

6. Discuss Santiago's relationship to other living things: people, fish, plant life, and birds. What do these relationships tell you about Santiago as a character?

7. Recall your expectations for the outcome of this novella when you finished reading the first section that preceded Santiago's departure

from land. Did you anticipate that he would or would not succeed in breaking his streak of bad luck by bringing a big fish to shore? Using specific evidence from the beginning of the novella, explain the reasons for your expectations and the way in which these expectations were or were not fulfilled.

8. Write an essay in which you explain those things that Manolin can learn from Santiago.

9. List the things that Manolin does for Santiago. Analyze Manolin's motives for helping Santiago. In your judgment, does Manolin neglect certain things he might do or say that would be helpful to Santiago?

10. Write a journal entry describing the next day in Santiago's life after the close of the novella. What has he learned from his three-day ordeal at sea? What will he do next? How will the residents of the village and other fishermen regard him? Keep your speculations as faithful as possible to the elements of character and setting established in *The Old Man and the Sea*.

11. Identify a very emotional, important incident in your life or a tragic event in the world around you. Now write a paragraph or more describing this event, using Hemingway's style. Describe the event without adverbs or adjectives to reveal your emotions or to suggest the reaction the reader should to have to this event. Select nouns and verbs carefully to convey the drama of the event, and use simple or compound sentences only.

12. Describe the contents of each of Santiago's dreams. What are the common elements of these dreams? What is signified by the novella's ending, with Santiago once again dreaming of lions?

Topics Relating the Text to Life

13. Analyze the methods Santiago uses to attempt to accomplish his goal. Write a journal entry in which you discuss what you can learn from Santiago's approach to a difficult task.

14. Describe Santiago's reaction to losing the big marlin. Now recall a time in your life when you have failed to gain something you worked hard to obtain. Compare and contrast your reactions with Santiago's. Can you learn anything from Santiago, or could Santiago learn something from you?

15. Think about an old person you know, perhaps a person you live with and who has affection for you. Write a journal entry in which you reflect upon (a) the things you can learn from an old person or (b) the things an older person needs from the younger people around him or her.

16. Consider the place of rituals in your life. These rituals may be formal religious rituals, such as Santiago's prayers, or informal rituals, such as Santiago's careful folding of his pants each night. Describe the elements of a formal or informal ritual in your own life and analyze why you participate in it and what you hope to gain from it.

17. People dream when they sleep, although not everyone remembers his or her dreams. Keep a dream journal for a week. Upon arising each morning, jot down what you remember of your dreams. Notice whether your dreams, like Santiago's, contain recurring images and situations. You can decide whether you want to keep the dream journal private or share it with another person.

Topics Focusing on This Text in Relation to Other Texts

18. Read *The Bear* by William Faulkner and write an essay in which you make point-by-point comparisons and contrasts between the characters of Manolin and Santiago and Ike McCaslin and Sam Fathers. What do the comparisons and contrasts between the older and younger characters tell you about the differences in the themes of these novellas?

19. Read one or more of the following works or other works representative of the genre identified here: (a) parables from the Bible; (b) fables by La Fontaine; (c) the allegory *Pilgrim's Progress* by John Bunyan; (d) an epic such as *The Odyssey* or *The Iliad*; or (e) tall tales such as those in George Washington Harris's *Sut Lovingood's Yarns*. Compare and contrast the plot, setting, and characters in the works(s) you have read with those elements in *The Old Man and the Sea*. Are the similarities or differences between Hemingway's novella and the work you have read more or less significant? What do these comparisons and contrasts tell you about the genre of *The Old Man and the Sea*?

20. Read the entire editorial in *Life* magazine of September 1952 and judge whether the events in Hemingway's life parallel events in *The Old Man and the Sea* in ways that make the novella more comprehensible to you. List the elements in *The Old Man and the Sea* that differ from those in Hemingway's life as described in the editorial.

21. Read Stephen Crane's short story "The Open Boat." Compare and contrast the plight of the men at sea in that story with Santiago's situation in *The Old Man and the Sea*. Examine as well the similarities and differences in Crane's and Hemingway's depiction of the sea. Explain why the definition of "naturalism" might be applied to "The Open Boat." Explain why the definition of "naturalism" can or cannot be applied to *The Old Man and the Sea*.

22. Hemingway's *The Old Man and the Sea* was made into a film starring Spencer Tracy. Produced by Warner Brothers, the movie was released in October 1958. This was Hemingway's twelfth work of fiction to be turned into a film but the only one in the production of which Hemingway was directly involved because he insisted that the producers render his novella faithfully. Watch the video of the 1958 film version of *The Old Man and the Sea* and respond to the following questions, which prompt you to explore the written text by comparing and contrasting it to the film version:

- Does Spencer Tracy fulfill well your expectations for the character of Santiago? Compare and contrast the specific physical traits and behavior of the character as presented in the novella with those of the actor in the film.

- Hemingway wanted the film to present an authentic setting, including real sharks and marlin—not Hollywood rubber fish. Evaluate the authenticity of the setting as it is depicted in the film, looking particularly at the scenes presenting Santiago at sea.

23. Read reviews of the 1958 film version of *The Old Man and the Sea* to determine reviewers' judgments of the film's fidelity to the written text. (See "Suggested Readings and Works Cited" at the end of this chapter for sources.) Is this fidelity an important criterion for judging the film according to these reviewers?

SUGGESTED READINGS AND WORKS CITED

Adair, William. "Eighty-five as a Lucky Number in *The Old Man and the Sea*." *Notes on Contemporary Literature* 8:1 (1978): 9.

Baker, Carlos. *Ernest Hemingway: A Life Story*. New York: Charles Scribner's Sons, 1969.

Brenner, Gerry. *The Old Man and the Sea: Story of a Common Man*. Twayne Masterwork Studies No. 89. New York: Twayne Publishers, 1991.

Fisher, James. *Spencer Tracy: A Bio-Bibliography*. Westport, CT: Greenwood Press, 1994.

Flora, Joseph. "Biblical Allusion in *The Old Man and the Sea*." *Studies in Short Fiction* 10 (1973): 143–47.

Hurley, C. Harold. "Just a 'Boy' or 'Already a Man'? Manolin's Age in *The Old Man and the Sea*." In *Hemingway's Debt to Baseball in* The Old Man and the Sea: *A Collection of Critical Readings*, ed. C. Harold Hurley. Lewiston, NY: Edwin Mellen Press, 1992. 95–101.

Jobes, Katherine, ed. *Twentieth Century Interpretations of* The Old Man and the Sea: *A Collection of Critical Essays*. Englewood Cliffs, NJ: Prentice Hall, 1968.

Johnson, Halverson. "Christian Resonance in *The Old Man and the Sea*." *English Language Notes* 2 (1964): 50–54.

Laurence, Frank M. *Hemingway and the Movies*. Jackson: University Press of Mississippi, 1981.

Losado, Luis, and Kathleen Morgan. "Santiago in *The Old Man and the Sea*: A Homeric Hero." *Hemingway Review* 12:1 (Fall 1992): 35–51.

Manning, Robert. "Hemingway in Cuba." *Atlantic Monthly* 216:2 (August 1965): 101–8.

Mellard, James. "Homer, Hemingway, and the Oral Tradition." *Style* (Spring 1992): 129–41.

Mellow, James R. *Hemingway: A Life Without Consequence*. Boston: Houghton Mifflin, 1992.

Meyers, Jeffrey. *Hemingway: A Biography*. New York: Harper & Row, 1985.

———, ed. *Hemingway: The Critical Tradition*. London: Routledge & Kegan Paul, 1982.

Oliver, Charles, ed. *A Moving Picture Feast: The Filmgoer's Hemingway*. New York: Praeger, 1989.

Phillips, Gene D. *Hemingway and Film*. New York: Frederick Ungar Publishing, 1980.

Plimpton, George. "The Art of Fiction, XXI: Ernest Hemingway: An Interview." *Paris Review* 18 (Spring 1958): 61–89.

Reynolds, Michael. *Hemingway: The Final Years*. New York: W. W. Norton, 1999.

Schorer, Mark. Review. *New Republic* 127 (6 October 1952): 19–20.

Timms, David. "Contrasts in Form: Hemingway's *The Old Man and the Sea* and Faulkner's *The Bear*." In *The Modern American Novella*, ed. Robert A. Lee. New York: St. Martin's Press, 1989. 97–112.

Thompson, Edward K. "Great American Storyteller." *Life* 33 (1 September 1952): 33.

Wilson, G. R. "Incarnation and Redemption in *The Old Man and the Sea*." *Studies in Short Fiction* 14 (1977): 369–73.

Young, Phillip. *Ernest Hemingway*. New York: Rinehart & Co., 1952.

Reviews of the 1958 film version of *The Old Man and the Sea* can be found in the following: *America* 100 (25 October 1958): 118; *BFI/ Monthly Film Bulletin* 26 (January 1959): 4; *Catholic World* 188 (November 1958): 151; Bosley Crowther, *New York Times*, 12 October 1958, 2: 1; *Film Daily* 113 (21 May 1958): 6; *Filmfacts* 1 (12 November 1958): 185–87; *Films in Review* 9 (August–September 1958): 396–98; Philip T.

Hartung, *Commonweal* 69 (3 October 1958): 16; *Hollywood Reporter* 10 (19 May 1958): 3; *Hollywood Reporter* 10 (January 1959): 1; *Hollywood Reporter* 10 (April 1959): 216; Stanley Kauffmann, *New Republic* 139 (6 October 1958): 21; Arthur Knight, *Saturday Review* 41 (4 October 1958): 26; *Library Journal* 83 (August 1958): 2150; *Life* 45 (6 October 1958): 124–29; *Look* 22 (2 September 1958): 66–67; *Newsweek* 51 (13 October 1958): 119; *New York Times* (5 October 1958): 2:7; *New Yorker* 34 (18 October 1958): 154; *Popular Photography* 43 (September 1958): 106–8; *Time* 72 (27 October 1958): 42; *Variety* (21 May 1958): 6.

2

The Cuban Environment: Geography and Climate and the Living Organisms They Support

The Old Man and the Sea incorporates many facets of Cuban geography, climate, and landscape—all elements of setting that influence Santiago's characterization as an impoverished man who earns his living at sea.

Located a mere ninety miles south of Florida, Cuba, the largest island in the West Indies, has a landmass that is generally flat or rolling, with the exception of the three mountain ranges found in the west, the center, and the southeastern part of the island. The Sierra del Cobre is part of the highest mountain range and the site of significant copper mining. (The word *cobre* means "copper.") The island's forests yield mahogany, ebony, and citrus trees, though in recent years, aggressive foresting has significantly reduced the number of these natural resources. Cuba's semitropical climate and landscape also support numerous species of palms, some of which supply the material for Santiago's hut, and the island is home to approximately 300 species of birds.

Cuba's coast is dotted with numerous gulfs and bays. Santiago lives in an unnamed fishing village that could plausibly be nestled in just such a bay, as is the village of Cojimar, the fishermen and ambience of which infused Hemingway's imagination as he wrote *The Old Man and the Sea*. Cuba's irregular coast also creates excellent harbors, including Matanzas, Guantánamo, Havana, and

Cuba and the surrounding waters, with sites relevant to the novella. Map by Sarah Lynn Brown.

Cienfuegos, the town from which Santiago's remembered arm wrestling competitor originated.

But Cuban geography does not end with its irregular coastline, for the waters surrounding this island nation are as important to it as its land. The Caribbean Sea lies to the south of Cuba, the Atlantic Ocean to the northeast, and the Gulf of Mexico to the northwest. The Straits of Florida stretch between the southernmost tip of the continental United States and the northernmost shore of Cuba. These waters are replete with almost 700 species of fish and crustaceans, and the abundance of marine life presented in *The Old Man and the Sea* further establishes the authenticity of its setting.

One marine organism, however, dominates the narrative in this novella: the marlin. This focus upon the marlin reflects the author's own obsession with that fish, and a student of the marlin in waters off Cuban shores would do well to refer to Hemingway's

The blue marlin is drawn to approximate the size of Santiago's catch, relative to the hawksbill turtle and the mako shark. Thus the marlin is drawn as if it were around 1,500 pounds in relation to the shark, which is drawn to represent the average seven-foot mako, and the hawksbill, which averages three feet in length. Drawing by Marie-Louise Locklear.

nonfiction writing on that subject. In several publications during the decades before he wrote *The Old Man and the Sea*, Hemingway documented various aspects of the marlin's appearance and behavior, as well as tips for fishermen who sought this big game.

Hemingway's most extensive and authoritative writing on marine life off Cuba, focusing on the marlin in particular, appeared in 1935 as a lengthy chapter in the prestigious book *American Big Game Fishing*. In his chapter, Hemingway provides a full description of the marlin's habits. Hemingway describes the process of fishing for marlin and classifies the ways in which a marlin will take the bait (in hunger or in anger, playfully or indifferently). Hemingway also identifies the characteristics of different types of marlin. The blue marlin off Cuba is a voracious feeder, Hemingway tells us, while the black marlin is a stupid fish, though an immensely powerful one that jumps magnificently. Then Hemingway details the fish's behavior after being hooked and recounts tactics for catching a marlin (61–73).

Hemingway also supplies a list of fish (81), in English and in Spanish, common to the deep-sea fisherman in the waters surrounding Cuba:

English	Spanish
broadbill	*imperador*
dolphin	*dorado*
goggle-eyes	*chicharros*
mackerel, cero: bait fish pintada	*pintada*
marlin, black	*pez grande* or *aguja negra*
marlin, blue	*azules* or *aguja bobos*
marlin, striped	*casteros* or *aguja de casta*
marlin, white	*aguja blanca*
mullet	*lisa*
pikelike fish	*guaguaucho*
pilchards	*machuelos*
tuna, albacore	*albacoras*
tuna, bonito	*bonitos*
shark, mako	*dentuso*

Although Hemingway's approach to fishing was that of a sportsman, he also knew of difficulties and challenges the marlin could pose for fishermen whose livelihood depended upon catching and bringing that fish to market. In "On the Blue Water," published in 1936, Hemingway recounted the experience of one such fisherman who had sailed into the Gulf of Mexico from the coastal village of Cabañas. This old fisherman had hooked an enormous marlin, which dragged the man in his small skiff sixty miles toward the Atlantic Ocean. The fisherman held on for the duration of one night, the next day, and the following night as well. Despite the fisherman's tenacity and his courageous battle against the sharks, using only his knife and oars, the magnificent catch was ravaged. The sharks' feasting upon the marlin reduced it to 800 pounds, approximately half its weight, according to Hemingway, who also recounts that when the fisherman was rescued at sea, he was crying hysterically (184). Obviously, many of the details of this incident suggest the basic elements of the plot of *The Old Man and the Sea*, but a key difference lies in the reaction of the fisherman, who is broken by his ordeal and his loss.

Because the quest for the marlin dominates the narrative structure of *The Old Man and the Sea*, a reader may not realize the scope of marine life included in that novella. This sheer abundance enhances all aspects of setting. Furthermore, Santiago's understanding and description of numerous marine organisms are yet another way that Hemingway delineates the character of his fisherman. Santiago's extensive knowledge establishes him firmly as a person whose entire life has been involved with and dependent upon the birds, fish, and plants that inhabit the waters off Cuba.

Precise scientific identification of all marine organisms named in *The Old Man and the Sea* is not possible because Santiago, true to his characterization, uses common names, not proper names, when referring to them. People who are not scientists usually do not use the proper, scientific names to identify the living organisms encountered daily, but scientists identify all organisms biologically by two names, one signifying their genus and the other their species. Although this dual system of naming in Latin, known as the "binomial nomenclature," creates a precise way to identify all living things, people rarely use this terminology in their everyday speech.

The following list places within the plant, animal, and fish kingdoms each of the marine organisms mentioned in the novella. The first column lists the organism's name (followed by the Spanish term, when applicable). The second column provides the organism's Latin name and some basic information about its scientific classification.

Common Name	**Scientific Name**
Marine plants	
Gulfweed, Sargasso Weed, Yellow Gulf Weed	*Sargassum natans*: multicellular algae in the division Phaeophyta (brown seaweeds)
Marine animals without backbones (invertebrates)	
Portuguese Man-of-War	*Physalia physalis*: invertebrate in the phylum Cnidaria (jellyfish, corals, sea anemones)
Squid	*Loligo sp.*: invertebrate in the phylum Mollusca (clams, oysters, octopi, squid)

Shrimp	*Penaeus sp*.: invertebrate in the phylum Arthropoda (insects, lobsters, horseshoe crabs, shrimp)

Marine animals with backbones (vertebates)

Mako (*dentuso*)	*Isurus sp.* (short-finned mako, *Isurus oxyrinchus*; long-finned mako, *Isurus paucus*): cartilaginous fish in the subclass Elasmobranchii (sharks, skates, rays), family Lamnidae (mackerel sharks)
Shovelnose (possibly the bignose; *galanos*)	*Carcharhinus altimus*: cartilaginous fish in the subclass Elasmobranchii (sharks, skates, rays), family Carcharhinidae (requiem sharks)
Flying fish	Family Exocoetidae: bony fish in the order Beloniformes (needlefish, flying fish)
Blue marlin	*Makaira nigricans*: bony fish in the order Perciformes, family Istiophoridae (sailfish, spearfish, marlin)
Barracuda	Family Sphyraenidae: bony fish in the order Mugiliformes
Tuna, albacore and bonito	*Thunnus alalunga* (albacore), *Sarda sarda* (bonito): bony fish in the family Scombridae (mackerels, tunas)
Sardine	*Sardinella sp*.: bony fish in the family Clupeidae (herrings, sardines)
Remora (sucking fish)	*Remora remora*: bony fish in the order Echiniformes, family Echeneididae
Pompano dolphin (dorado)	*Coryphaena equisetis*: bony fish in the order Perciformes, family Coryphaenidae
Sea turtles	Family Cheloniidae (green turtle, *Chelonia mydas*; hawksbill, *Eretmochelys imbricata*; leatherback, *Dermochelys coriacea*; loggerhead, *Caretta caretta*): reptiles in the order Chelonia (turtles)
Tern	*Sterna sp*.: seabird in the order Ciconiiformes, family Laridae (gulls, terns)
Frigatebird (robber bird)	*Fregata sp*.: seabird in the order Ciconiiformes, family Fregatidae (frigatebirds)

Storm-petrel (sea swallow)   *Oceanites sp.*: seabird in the order Ci-
                                     coniiformes, family Procellariidae (pet-
                                     rels, shearwaters, albatross, storm-
                                     petrels)

In addition to his knowledge of marine organisms, Santiago is
aware of signals in the weather. The subtropical Cuban climate is
generally kind to the island's inhabitants, but the weather can turn
cruel in hurricane season, and Santiago knows this. Lacking the
sophisticated weather forecasting that now allows people to prepare for or to flee a hurricane's fury, Santiago relies upon his observation of the sky and clouds to alert him to this potential
disaster. He is confident that no hurricane is near, even though he
is at sea during September, the worst month for hurricanes.

The documents that follow allow the reader to understand the
ways in which Cuban geography and climate are used as significant
elements in the setting for *The Old Man and the Sea*. Cuban climate and landscape are by all accounts beautiful and inviting, as
the famed naturalist Thomas Barbour demonstrates. The weather
is moderate, but Cuba's climate can also produce seasonal threats
in the form of hurricanes, about which Santiago is conscious and
vigilant. Natural resources on both land and sea have provided
Cubans with pleasures and a livelihood; the scope of these resources, specifically in the area of marine organisms off Cuba's
coast, can be more fully appreciated when we view Hemingway's
depiction of them through the eyes of Bonnie Kelley, a professor
of biology, who applies her expertise and experience to the novella. Robert P. Weeks, however, takes a very different approach to
Hemingway's treatment of marine life, specifically his treatment of
the marlin. As a literary critic, Weeks has a perspective derived from
his knowledge of Hemingway's avowed desire to achieve realism
in all his writing. Weeks takes Hemingway to task for any exaggeration or lack of plausibility in presenting this fish and its habits.

CUBAN CLIMATE AND LANDSCAPE

Thomas Barbour, a renowned naturalist, traveled to Cuba numerous times before his death in 1946. His descriptions of the myriad species of wildlife that inhabit Cuban forests, mountains, and surrounding waters, as well as his accounts of many aspects of Cuban geography and landscape, attest to both the beauty of the island and his own affection for it. Excerpts from Barbour's book have been reprinted in a variety of sources.

The following excerpt provides details of Cuban climate and weather, which is generally pleasant, even in the hottest months. We know that Santiago is unafraid to be out of sight of land, even in September—the month of hurricanes and the month in which the novella is set—because he is confident in his ability to read the signs supplied by sky, cloud, and wind. Barbour's explanation of the northers and hurricanes puts these phenomena in a fearful context, one that Santiago appears not to experience.

FROM THOMAS BARBOUR, *A NATURALIST IN CUBA*

(Boston: Little, Brown, and Co., 1945)

Cuba is, generally speaking, a hot country with a very uniform temperature. The rainfall is distributed as in so many tropical regions, there being a rainy season and a dry. From May to November it is rainy and from December to April dry. The rainy season is normally marked by two peaks of rainfall—usually in June and October. The summer season is characterized by frequent thunderstorms. These are preceded by the formation of magnificent castles of towering cumulus clouds, accompanied by the dying out of the breezes until the heat becomes extremely oppressive; then comes what the Cubans call the *aire de agua*, a fresh, humid, and most agreeable breath of air. The thunder now increases to drum-fire intensity, the lightning flashes sometimes almost unceasingly. Finally the skies open and rain falls in a way that we seldom see it fall here in the North. Cloudbursts of a number of inches falling in a single hour are not unusual.

Two phenomena are so characteristic and dramatic that I cannot pass them by without a word. I recall the first of many northers which I have felt and seen in Havana. A norther is usually preceded by a south wind. Perhaps you know the old saying: *A Sur duro, Norte seguro*. The south wind gradually dies out and there is a breathless stillness which somehow always seems to me to convey, subconsciously, an aura of impending trouble. Suddenly the norther, really a northwester, starts to blow; the temperature drops and there may be a drizzle or a sharp shower of rain. If you are in Havana my advice is to hurry to the Malacón and watch the ocean grow angry. If the norther is a really bad one you'll soon have to take shelter. Many a time have I seen the waves rise to dash and break, the spray flying over the lighthouse on Morro Castle. I have often seen the streets of the waterfront inundated in a few hours after the onset of the storm and when the tempest has died away seen gangs of workmen clearing away rifts of sand and coral heads tossed up by the waves into the streets. The weather now may clear and then a few days of fresh, cool weather ensue, most enjoyable wherever you may be. Sometimes, however, the succeeding days of cold may bring great suffering to people who live in houses where there is no glass in the windows and no blankets on the beds. The northers are the exciting feature of winter weather and they form a contrast to the hurricanes of the summer months.

So far as I know no really good explanation for the origin of a hurricane has ever been determined. To say that they are tornadoes or twisters on a giant scale is descriptive but not explanatory. Cyclones usually build themselves up in the ocean east of the Caribbean Sea, frequently blow across Cuba and pass out over Yucatán, or blow along Cuba and perhaps strike the Mexican coast, sometimes curling back to Florida. Many others, however, miss Cuba entirely, crossing the Bahama Islands to strike Florida, or curving northward to reach the coast of Virginia and even New England. The latent powers within the atmosphere are impossible to describe. One day may be calm, peaceful, and the next the elements may rage with such force and engendering such terror that it is almost impossible to describe. The sight of the oncoming hurricane is awe-inspiring. The noise of the rising wind is fearful. The sheer heights of fury which it reaches at the peak of the storm are indescribable, and overwhelming. I don't mind anyone's saying that he has been afraid during a hurricane. I don't believe any living person has ever passed through one and not been afraid. The sights of buildings and villages blowing to pieces, of the tops of palm trees popping off and hurtling over the ground like tumbleweeds on the prairie, is a manifestation of the power of nature which is unequaled. I am sure the typhoons in the Old World may be just as bad as the hurricanes in the New, but my own experience has done nothing but make me hope and pray quite simply and humbly that I may never see one again. (261–64)

MARINE ORGANISMS

Dr. Bonnie Kelley has a bachelor of science in biology from North Georgia College, a master's degree in science education from the University of Georgia, and a doctorate in plant pathology from the University of Georgia. She has had training in oceanography from San Diego State University and has co-taught a course in marine biology, taking students to Bermuda to provide a field laboratory. Dr. Kelley teaches the plant, fish, and bird facets of this course. Because the plot of *The Old Man and the Sea* is dominated by Santiago's quest for the marlin, readers may not focus upon or appreciate the richness of other marine life depicted in that novella. But Dr. Kelley's perspective alerts us to the fullness of Hemingway's presentation of all aspects of the marine environment—from its turtles and sargasso weed to migrating birds and phosphorescent patches of sea. Dr. Kelley is an award-winning teacher, who points out many possibilities for interdisciplinary study and research stemming from a reading of the novella. She was the recipient of the North Carolina Board of Governor's Award for Teaching Excellence in 1995, the first year that award was established.

INTERVIEW WITH DR. BONNIE KELLEY

(26 June 2001)

PV: I'd like to begin the interview on anything that you want to say about the marine organisms in this novella and your judgment on how they are presented.

BK: The marine organisms in the book are, I think, portrayed extremely well. And there's a good variety of them to give the reader a feel for the sea and all of the complexity of that particular environment. This would be an excellent book for an interdisciplinary science/ English project for students. I am impressed with Hemingway's portrayal of the organisms.

PV: I was struck by some things that you had brought out to me in earlier conversations. I hadn't really paid attention to the turtles in advance of our conversation. Could you talk about the different kinds of turtles and how they are portrayed?

BK: I was very interested in [Hemingway's] talking about the three kinds of turtles that Santiago identifies as green turtles, loggerheads, and the hawksbills. Basically, [Hemingway] portrays the green turtle and the hawksbill as being more noble organisms than the logger-head. . . .

PV: Santiago apparently goes turtling in addition to fishing. Do you know anything about that?

BK: Well, turtle meat is really prized, and turtles are much easier to catch than fish. Many of these turtles grow to be extremely large, and sailing ships would actually run into them. Turtles could be kept on board for a period of time as a food source. . . .

PV: So, one could catch a turtle and hold on to it until needed. A turtle obviously is not like a fish, which will die out of water and must be gutted or preserved.

BK: [Nods in agreement.]

PV: What about the birds?

BK: Birds are some of my favorite marine organisms. Santiago comments that seabirds have a hard life. Seabirds swoop down, plunging from the sky into the water, going after something that they have seen up there and are trying to gauge—hit-and-miss. They are going from one medium to another medium and trying to get enough to eat.

PV: Going between air and sea is going from one medium to another. That's an interesting way to put it. Santiago also says that evening or dusk is a difficult time for fish. Does that have any factual basis?

BK: Sharks are somewhat different [fish] because many of them are night creatures, and they basically do not depend much on sight. They depend primarily on smell. They have very poor eyesight. Most fish, however, look for a place to hide and sleep protected during the night because they are dependent on light primarily. Fish [feed] in upper regions of the water, where light can penetrate. At dusk, [most fish] would have difficulty if they have not gotten their food complement for the day, and they would also be more vulnerable to predators [such as sharks].

PV: Because sharks don't depend upon sight the way other fish do. What about shark attacks? Are they the exception to the rule rather than the actual rule of the shark's behavior?

BK: Santiago contrasts the mako, for whom he has great respect because he is a predator, to the shovelnose, which [Santiago] says is a scav-

enger. [Santiago] doesn't like the behavior of the shovelnose because he says when a shovelnose is hungry, he'll bite anything. He'll
go after humans, the oars of a boat. And Santiago doesn't respect
this way to gain nutrition.

PV: That's a very interesting point, and I'm so glad you made it, because
it fits in with the whole ethos of the sportsmanship that pervades
this novella. It isn't simply obtaining the goal, the win, the fish, the
catch. It's how one goes about it. So you're saying that Santiago has
respect for the more sportsmanlike of the sharks.

BK: Yes, Another interesting point to me was how Santiago puts himself
in the scheme of nature. I think that's an important thing this book
can do for young students; our culture is separated from the way
their food source comes to them. I mean, they see it on a grocery
store counter, and they don't see beyond how that food was processed, how that food was killed. The Bible says man has dominion
over all of the animals and the plants, and I think that we need to
look at that statement instead of saying we should control everything that is here on earth. Maybe we need to look at humans as
being part of the natural process. And I think if we can get young
students to do that, they will have a different attitude toward pol-
luting the earth, toward the use of the animals for furs and frivolous
things like that. This book can contribute to getting the student back
in touch with the fact that man has to fit into the ecosystem.

PV: I also noticed that when Santiago kills the dolphin for the purpose
of the food, he tosses the carcass overboard. That would put blood
in the water, right? Now, when the shark is looking for prey, if he
doesn't rely on sight, does blood attract?

BK: It's primarily the smell. The shark relies on smell. You know blood
has a very, very strong odor that would not be mistaken for anything
else. Santiago, when he catches the fish, takes off what he thinks he
needs for his own sustenance. Returning the carcass to the sea is
recycling to feed another animal. Dead things settle very quickly.
The problem with the marlin tied to Santiago's boat is that it is
constantly in the upper regions. [The marlin] would draw the predator right to [the boat]. Putting the carcass [of the dolphin in the
sea] and moving away from it was not a threat to Santiago in the
boat. He was returning that part of what he caught back to the
system.

PV: I wondered when I first read the novella if there was anything Santiago might have done to have prevented [the shark attack]. But I
guess he really had no choice because he couldn't keep that carcass

in the boat with him. He didn't describe what he did with the carcass of the tunas that he had caught. . . .

BK: [Santiago] watches the carcass [of the dolphin] descend into the water, and he uses its descent as an indication of how much more [day]light he has according to the depth at which he can still see the carcass.

You can study the ocean in levels. There's the level where there's light, and light will only go down so far, and if a fish is dependent on that light, it's got to have some type of buoyancy device to keep in that level.

Some fish use muscle power, and they must keep swimming. [The shark is in this category.] Some fish use air pockets to get the buoyance that they need to stay in the level. And most fish have swim bladders. They can actually rise vertically, oxygen passes in through the gills; they feed it down into the swim bladder to change their level.

PV: What is the name for the light zone and the zone below light?

BK: Photic zone and aphotic zone; there's no light there.

Plants are the basis of all food chains, whether on land or in the water. And, of course, plants make the initial source of food using sunlight, a process called "photosynthesis." Basically, if there is plankton [the aggregate of those floating, drifting organisms in the water], there are little fish. Santiago refers to the plankton; he recognizes that the sea water is cloudy, . . . and he knows that there is life there, and he knows that microscopic life is going to bring a lot of fish because of the way the [food] chain works. So he is very aware that there are areas in the ocean that are very productive, and this is where one needs to fish.

He talks about a deep hole as he's rowing out of the harbor. He mentions an area that becomes very deep, and, in marine talk, that would be called an "undersea canyon"; the current rubbing against the sides of that undersea hole stirs things up. In the ocean, if things aren't stirred up, everything settles because, as we've said, nonliving particles have no way to stay up. So this [current] stirs up oxygen and nutrient materials on the bottom. Santiago says this is an area that lots of fishermen want to fish because of those currents in that deep area.

Of course, Santiago's going farther out; he's after the big fish. He talks about weather, he talks about currents, the Gulf Stream, and the study of the Gulf Stream is just a wonderful study for any kind of science project.

PV: What wonderful things could one understand studying the Gulf Stream?

BK: The gulfweed itself.

PV: Is that distinct from the sargasso weed?

BK: That is the sargasso weed. At one point in the book, Santiago realizes he needs some sustenance. So he takes his can and pulls in a big clump of the gulfweed, and he shakes out these little shrimp—also good food—and eats them, and he says they are very nutritious.

The floating algae follow the Gulf Stream and provide a home for literally hundreds of organisms. If those shrimp fall off the gulfweed, where are they going? They are going down, and they are going to be food for something on the way down. So the gulfweed is a whole community in itself. Not only those shrimp live there, but gulfweed provides a nursery for tiny fish, if you like. You can find all kinds of little sea worms and organisms that are attached to it; . . . little "feather worms," they are called. They build a little home for themselves, and the way they feed is that they stick their little feathery antennae out, and they catch microscopic organisms. On a piece of gulfweed, there is a whole community of life. Everything in the community is on the weed, and the weed is not good to eat. It has chemicals in it that deter animals from eating it; they would be eating their home.

PV: Is the word "host" appropriate here?

BK: Yes. Without the weed, none of those organisms could exist.

PV: The photic, or light, zone is where the sargasso weed exists. Then there is the aphotic zone. Is there a third zone?

BK: When you're talking about light, there are only two zones: photic and aphotic. Ocean water will also layer itself according to temperature and salinity.

You may have heard of something called the "thermocline." That area where the temperature drastically changes is called a thermocline. Above the thermocline, the water is warmest at the top. Below, the water is very cold; the water down below the thermocline becomes around four degrees very quickly and remains at four degrees centigrade all the time.

PV: So, the temperature zone and the photic zone are related very closely?

BK: They're related because the sun-warmed water rises. So they are related but not necessarily exactly the same level.

PV: And the other layer?

BK: Salinity.

PV: Salinity, based on how much salt there is?

BK: Based on how much salt there is.

PV: And where is the greater amount of salt, top or bottom?

BK: The greater amount of salt would be in the top ranges because of the source of that salt—rivers pouring into the ocean, pouring in mineral materials. The salt is concentrated by evaporation. So you've got the source coming in at the top and evaporation concentrating that salt material, so you'll have salt water or saline water at the top.

PV: And, of course, this is important for Santiago because when he eats the fish, he is getting some saline based on the raw fish that he is eating, but he also wishes that he had some salt to cure the raw fish because it's so unpalatable.

BK: He's doesn't realize until too late that during the daytime he could have splattered the salt water up on top of the boat, and it would have evaporated and left the salt.

PV: I want to ask you about the marlin, specifically Santiago's attribution to the marlin of certain characteristics. On page 41 of *The Old Man and the Sea*, Santiago gets a hit, and he thinks to himself, "One hundred fathoms down a marlin was eating the sardines." How does this fit with the idea that fish need light to feed and hence feed in the photic zone?

BK: Most fish feed in the upper layers; due to its size, mobility, and speed, the marlin inhabits a much larger range.

PV: It has been disputed that no one could know that it is specifically a *marlin* that has taken the bait. But Santiago does stipulate that it's one hundred fathoms down. Can you comment at all on whether or not it is absurd or poetic license to say something like, "one hundred fathoms down a marlin had taken the sardines"?

BK: I don't think it's absurd at all because this man has been fishing all his life. He has tremendous experience, and he talks earlier about how meticulous he is about keeping all of his lines vertical and at the correct depth. Santiago talks about some of the younger fishermen. They think the [line's] at one hundred fathoms, and it's actually at sixty. He's very, very meticulous about his lines; . . . he talks about how [the line] feels, and he's using his hands. He's not holding a pole; he's holding that line in his hand, and basically, I think with his experience, knowing what could be that big and what he's more likely to catch at this level, I don't think it's absurd at all. He could identify pretty carefully what it was.

PV: There's another thing that Hemingway's been taken to task for allowing his character to think. Santiago remembers having hooked a female marlin, claiming that males always let the females eat first. Santiago says that the male marlin stayed by her side until she was gaffed. The sight saddened Santiago, and the narration of this incident implies a monogamous pairing of these fish. Do you know anything about that in terms of plausibility?

BK: I have to say, I do not. I would suspect that Hemingway had heard fishermen talk about this type of behavior. Students might find this an interesting animal behavior research project.

PV: Can you tell me where someone would go to do this type of research?

BK: Well, you'd have to find libraries that carry large, not only marine, collections, but animal behavior collections. Most of the marine stations around the world have extensive libraries where they have collected books and journals over the years.

PV: Let's use this idea of the marlin pairing for life to consider how Santiago fits himself into the whole world of living things. Making the marlin a monogamous pair is an anthropomorphism demonstrating how he connects on a level with what he had to do in nature.

I thought it was really interesting to discover how late in the novella the kill of the marlin actually comes. . . . We only have about twenty pages left for all the shark attacks, which I counted to be five. I was surprised by the number of shark attacks. It's page 94 where Santiago kills the marlin. He talks about the ways in which the blood oozes out of him and goes down for a mile. And I think that's another thing that's really very interesting, returning to what you said earlier about the sharks—how the blood is going to attract them enormously. And then with the marlin lashed to the side of the boat, he has created—

BK: A trail for them to follow.

PV: Yes. So, really, is there any possible way there could be an alternative scenario? He's out so far. He can't get the marlin in the boat because he's so enormous. Given the waters he is in, would there be any possible way he could get this marlin back to shore without a shark attack? And there are five separate attacks! This is a relentless, repeated thing!

BK: And, you know, they come until they eventually take it all. They've left the spine, the head, and probably the skull part. It would be more difficult for them to get the meat off the tail.

PV: The great tail!

BK: And they take all of the usable parts. As far as Santiago has traveled, you would expect the shark to come.

PV: So if you know these waters and anything about marine life, you also know that at the moment Santiago kills the marlin and lashes it to his boat, the sharks are going to come. The marlin's going to be savaged, ravaged, torn apart; it's not going to make it back to shore.

Bonnie, is there anything else you feel we haven't covered that you'd like to speak about?

BK: I wanted to say something about the little bird.

PV: The little bird?

BK: Yes. Santiago has the fish, and he's got the line across his shoulder, and all of a sudden there's a tiny little bird [identified as a warbler (p. 54)] that comes and first lights on the stern of the boat and then gets on the actual line. A tired little bird, Santiago calls him, and he talks to the bird about rest. This, too, could be a study for a student as to what type of bird it might be.

Birds migrate great distances, but they usually stop and sleep at night and rest. Over water, of course, the bird cannot light if it is not a seabird that can float on water. So this is a bird that is crossing a body of water, maybe migrating from south Florida to Cuba, and the boat provides a resting spot, and the little bird sits and rests. And he tells the bird that he should rest because as he approaches land, there are going to be hawks that are expecting little tired birds. And then the fish lurches [and that tugs at the line], and when Santiago looks, the bird is gone.

PV: Oh, interesting.

BK: It's just a neat little story of the peril that birds face when they are crossing large bodies of water. And you see another part of the whole web of life.

PV: The little bird creates a parallel, a leitmotiv in the story of Santiago and the marlin. Crossing this great body of water, there are all sorts of difficulties, such as fatigue and natural predators.

Is there anything else that we should notice regarding marine life in *The Old Man and the Sea*?

BK: Santiago talks about the phosphorescence.

PV: Oh, yes. When he urinates off the boat, he notices phosphorescence in the water.

BK: What's happening there is there are microscopic organisms in the water that can produce light. And there are areas in the Caribbean where these organisms grow.

Basically, if you go out on the ocean at night, you can see it. There are cycles. It would be an interesting study to see where and in what context there is phosphorescence. And Santiago realizes that phosphorescence is the presence of organisms. He says that the gulfweed actually glows at one point. That would be a good point for a student to research: Is the phosphorescence coming from the actual gulfweed itself or from organisms using the gulfweed?

PV: Your comment also suggests another possibility for research. Might a student be able to determine Santiago's location based on phosphorescent sites?

BK: Well, they are actually small algae, organisms that have mechanisms that allow them to rise in a water column at night. There have been studies many, many times about the cycle of these photosynthetic organisms; they need to be up in the photic zone when there is light up there. They will rise during the night, photosynthesize at early morning, and then they will sink back down into the water column. If you were a student of the ocean, as Santiago was, you could even determine whether it was midnight or early in the evening based upon an understanding of phosphorescence. Santiago is aware of the phosphorescence, and he can use that to give him a better chance at night. He can gauge how much time he has before sunlight, for example.

PV: Something as subtle as a description of phosphorescence is so meaningless to a person who knows nothing about it, but it becomes so meaningful to a student of marine organisms, such as yourself.

BK: Maybe the science students and the English students could teach each other all kinds of stuff.

"FAKERY" IN PRESENTING THE FACTS OF A FISHERMAN'S EXPERIENCES IN *THE OLD MAN AND THE SEA*

Critics of Hemingway's writing are so accustomed to the writer's fidelity to actual real-world detail that one scholar in particular was incensed to detect discrepancies between Hemingway's nonfictional and fictional accounts of Cuban fishermen and their feats of fishing for marlin in the Gulf of Mexico. In the following excerpt from Robert P. Weeks's article "Fakery in *The Old Man and the Sea*," the title reveals that critic's judgment of Hemingway's use of Cuban material. Notice how Weeks compares and contrasts Hemingway's statements in essays published in *American Big Game Fishing* and *Esquire* with his depiction of the habits of marlin and the experiences of real Cuban commercial fishermen at the time of *The Old Man and the Sea*'s composition. Weeks refers to the incident Hemingway recounted in "On the Blue Water," summarized above, and provides facts supplied by authorities such as ichthyologists, experts on fish, at the University of Miami Marine Laboratory and the American Museum of Natural History to inform the reader about the habits of marlin in the Gulf of Mexico. Weeks focuses his attention on Hemingway's depiction of the marlin and fishing for them. He does not analyze or judge Hemingway's portrayal of the myriad other forms of marine life that populate the novella. The excerpt begins with Weeks's commenting on Santiago's claim to know, when he first feels the tug of a fish on his line, that this fish is a marlin.

FROM ROBERT P. WEEKS, "FAKERY IN *THE OLD MAN AND THE SEA*"

(*College English* 24 [December 1962])

This is not fishing skill; it's clairvoyance. The signals that can be transmitted over a pencil-thick line dangling more than six hundred feet into the ocean are relatively gross. Moreover, as Hemingway himself points out in his essay "Marlin Off Cuba," in *American Big Game Fishing*, published in an elegant limited edition of 906 copies by the Derrydale Press in 1935, one cannot tell whether the fish taking his bait is a marlin or a broadbill for they "take the bait in much the same manner, first, perhaps picking off a few of the sardines with which the point of the hook is covered, then seizing the whole fish used as bait between their jaws to crush it a moment before swallowing it."

This hint that Hemingway may be padding his characterization of Santiago by means of fakery is abundantly confirmed by the action that follows. His combat with the fish is an ordeal that would do in even a vigorous young man. He is at sea nearly four full days, almost all of that time without sleep and during much of it hanging onto a 1,500-pound fish that steadily tows him and his boat for miles, most of it *against* the current of the Gulf Stream. At noon on the third day, the giant fish circles the boat and the old man harpoons it, lashes it to the boat, and sets sail for home. Almost at once the sharks attack the fish, and the old man attacks the sharks. He battles them for more than twelve hours, quitting only when he runs out of weapons. Then, competently—and evidently without sleeping—he sails his little skiff for his home port, arriving shortly before dawn.

The extent to which this is an incredible performance is made clear when we turn to Hemingway himself for some notion of how an actual old Cuban fisherman behaved under similar circumstances. In "On the Blue Water," an essay that appeared in *Esquire* in 1936, Hemingway wrote:

> Another time an old man fishing alone in a skiff out of Cabanas hooked a giant marlin that, on the heavy sashcord handline, pulled the skiff far out to sea. Two days later the old man was picked up by fishermen sixty miles to the eastward, the head and forward part of the marlin lashed alongside. . . . He was crying in the boat when the fishermen picked him up, half crazy from his loss, and the sharks were still circling the boat.

It is hardly surprising that Santiago's clairvoyancy also enables him to be an uncanny meteorologist. While he is being towed by his fish, he looks at the sky, then soliloquizes: "If there is a hurricane you always see signs of it in the sky for days ahead, if you are at sea. They do not see it ashore because they do not know what to look for." Scientists on land, sea, and in the air equipped with delicate pressure-sensing devices and radar cannot duplicate the powers that Hemingway off-handedly—and unconvincingly—gives to Santiago. According to the Chief District Meteorologist of the United States Weather Bureau in Miami, Florida, Gordon E. Dunn, "It is usually impossible to see signs of a tropical storm for more than two days in advance and on occasion it is difficult to tell for sure that there is a tropical storm in the vicinity for even a day in advance."

But it is when Santiago's fish makes its first appearance that the fakery truly begins to flow. For example, the old man perceives at once that it is a male. Hemingway heroes almost always measure themselves against male animals, whether they are kudu, lions, bear, bulls, or fish. The tragedy enacted in the bull ring becomes a farce if you replace the bull with a cow. The hunter, the torero, the fisherman prove that *they* have *cojones* by engaging another creature that has them beyond dispute. Santiago's marlin is both huge and possessed of incredible endurance. He tows man and boat for nearly three days.

But the marlin presents problems. Its *cojones* are internal. "The sexes are not recognizable in these animals except by internal dissection," according to Gilbert Voss, an ic[h]thyologist with the University of Miami Marine Laboratory. Confronted by this dilemma—by the need to pit his hero against a male fish on the one hand, but a fish whose sex he won't be able to determine by dissection before the sharks devour all the evidence, on the other—Hemingway resorts to the fakery of having Santiago identify him at once as a male. In an effort, perhaps, to make this bit of fakery more believable, Hemingway has Santiago recall an experience with marlin in which he was able to distinguish the male from the female. . . .

Santiago's story of the devoted male marlin actually creates more problems than it solves. It is a preposterous piece of natural history, combining sentimentality and inexact observation. The Associate Curator of Fishes of the American Museum of Natural History, who was also a friend of Hemingway's, Francesca LaMonte, noticed an interesting parallel between Santiago's story and one Hemingway recounts in his marlin essay in *American Big Game Fishing*. . . . Miss LaMonte comments on this story that "You will note that the sex of the other fishes is not stated." Hemingway has Santiago incredibly enough identify the uncaught fish as males but in his essay he is more realistic.

Santiago and his fish are yoked by Hemingway's method of using the animal to epitomize some aspect of the man. The result, as Carlos Baker admiringly puts it, is "gallantry against gallantry." It is in fact more nearly fakery against fakery: a make-believe super-fish duelling a make-believe super-fisherman. . . . It must be conceded that leaving aside these two formidable adversaries, there are brilliant flashes of Hemingway realism in *The Old Man and the Sea*. The sharks, for example, are depicted with remarkable vividness as they rush the dead marlin and savagely tear it apart. The shovel-nosed sharks with their "wide, flattened, shovel-pointed heads . . . and their slitted yellow cat-like eyes" are made "good and true enough" so that they are convincing as sharks *and* as embodiments of pure evil.

With the mako shark, however, Hemingway has not wholly resisted the impulse to fake. He has claimed for the mako that he can swim "as fast as the fastest fish in the sea" and equipped him with eight rows of teeth "shaped like a man's fingers when they are crisped like claws. They were nearly as long as . . . fingers . . . and they had razor-sharp cutting edges on both sides." E. M. Schroeder, of the Harvard Museum of Comparative Zoology, an authority on the sharks of the Atlantic, and other shark experts seriously doubt that the mako is as fast as the fastest fish. And they find support from Hemingway who in an article in *Game Fish of the World* says that the mako can "run faster than most," and in another article mentions the tuna and wahoo as "the fastest fish in the sea."

To describe the mako as having eight rows of teeth, as Hemingway does, is a great deal like saying that a five-year-old child has forty or so teeth. Only two rows of the shark's teeth are functional; the others are replacements which become functional as the forward teeth are lost or destroyed. Also, according to Professor Voss, only the main teeth in the mid part of the shark's jaw are as long, slender, and sharp as Hemingway describes *all* the teeth as being. Just as Santiago and his fish are given extraordinary powers they could not in fact possess, the biggest and most dangerous of the sharks, the mako, is made more menacing than he actually is. (188–91)

TOPICS FOR WRITTEN OR ORAL EXPLORATION

1. Santiago's catch of a gigantic marlin is lost to sharks. Another risk to the success of his fishing expedition might have been posed by the weather. September is a month when hurricanes are possible around Cuba and in the waters in which Santiago was fishing. Write an essay in which you describe the onset and elements of a hurricane and suggest how Hemingway might have introduced such a storm into his narrative. Conclude your essay with speculation about the consequences to the plot of *The Old Man and the Sea* had Santiago encountered a hurricane.

2. Relocate the events in *The Old Man and the Sea* to another place, perhaps a small village on the coast of New England during the 1950s. What elements of setting would need to be changed? How would the climate and marine organisms differ? What would commercial fishermen try to catch? What risks and challenges might these fishermen face? Reading Sebastian Junger's *The Perfect Storm* for the purposes of comparison might be useful.

3. Read Hemingway's articles on fishing off the Cuban shores. Compare and contrast Hemingway's presentation of marine life in these articles and in the novella. Does this exercise demonstrate Hemingway's fidelity in the novella to the facts he knew, or do departures from these facts in the novella have some narrative or thematic purpose in *The Old Man and the Sea*?

4. Consider the issue of realism in presenting the setting and the plausibility of events that could occur in that setting. Using evidence from the interview with Dr. Kelley and the excerpt from Weeks's article, write an essay in which you argue for or against the premise that Hemingway stays faithful to what is plausible for the marine organisms described in his novella.

5. Having begun his writing career as a reporter, Hemingway continued to write for various newspapers and periodicals over the course of his life. A reporter collects information and attempts to present it without distortion, embellishment, or exaggeration. Read some of Hemingway's nonfiction writing on fishing. Then, using evidence from the novella and from Hemingway's articles on the subject of fishing, debate whether or not Hemingway's presentation of information in *The Old Man and the Sea* is more reportorial or more fictional.

6. Refer to the list of living organisms presented in *The Old Man and the Sea*. One living organism is conspicuously absent: Santiago. Where would the fisherman fit in this outline? Santiago's remark to

the little bird, "Then go in and take your chance like any man or bird or fish" (55), implies that he thinks of himself as on the same level as the other living organisms, linking as he does himself by a simple conjunction to the bird and the fish. Write an essay in which you argue the point made by Dr. Kelley that this book can help readers to understand that humans should not use the natural world frivolously or carelessly. Use evidence from *The Old Man and the Sea* to support your claim.

7. "Anthropomorphism" is the attribution of human characteristics to a nonhuman being. The word is frequently used in a religious context to denote the attribution of human characteristics to divine beings, but anthropomorphisms can also occur with this kind of attribution to the animal or plant kingdoms. Argue for or against the premise that *The Old Man and the Sea* anthropomorphizes marine organisms. Think specifically about Santiago's comments about the turtle, the shark, and the marlin. Use evidence from the text to support your claim. You may also need to refer to scientific sources that document the behavior of marine organisms.

8. In an essay, assess the thematic import of either the turtles or the little bird to *The Old Man and the Sea*. Begin your essay by summarizing the text's presentation of the turtles or the little bird; then explain how the situations described have any similarities to plot or character. Conclude your essay with a statement of how the novella would be different if these organisms had not been included.

9. "Local color" is a term that applies to literature that emphasizes setting in order to illustrate the distinctive characteristics of a specific location. Landscape and geography are central to regional depiction, as is the portrayal of customs and dialect. Local color is a term most often applied to late-nineteenth-century writing about the American South, West, and Northeast. Argue for or against the application of the term "local color" to *The Old Man and the Sea*, considering the novella's detailed incorporation of marine organisms specific to the Cuban geography.

10. "Ecocriticism," a term that emerged at the end of the twentieth century, examines how a work of literature presents the physical environment. Setting is the basis for this examination, but the critic focuses upon the way in which the author and characters value the natural world and humans' place in it. Cheryll Glotfelty, in her introduction to *The Ecocriticism Reader*, says that students who take environmental literature courses will be encouraged to think about "the relationship of humans to nature, about the ethical and aesthetic dilemmas posed by the environmental crisis, and about how language

and literature transmit values with profound ecological implications" (xxv). Using part or all of Glotfelty's statement, analyze *The Old Man and the Sea*. What kind of an environmental statement does the novella make? How does it situate human beings within the environment? What kind of relationship exists between Santiago and the natural world? How does Hemingway present the numerous other life-forms in the novella?

11. Even though Santiago makes his living as a fisherman, he reveres the fish he must inevitably kill, apologizing to one at the moment of its death. He addresses the marlin he has hooked directly, telling him that though he loves and respects him, he will kill him. Other important works of American fiction explore the professional fisherman's quest and his relationship to the marine organisms in his geographical location. Compare and contrast this quest, as it is described in the quotations below, with Santiago's catch of the big marlin. Consider in your analysis the physical location and time in which each work of fiction is set. (You may wish to read the entire novel from which these quotations are taken.)

• From James Fenimore Cooper's *The Pioneers*, set in the late eighteenth century: Local fishermen are hauling enormous numbers of fish, mostly bass, onto the shores of Otsego Lake in upstate New York. The area's leading citizen, Temple Marmaduke, comments on the scene to his daughter, Bess:

> Fishes of various sorts now were to be seen, entangled in the meshes of the net, as it was passed through the hands of the labourers; and the water, at a little distance from the shore, was alive with the agitated movements of the alarmed victims. Hundreds of white sides were glancing up to the surface of the water, and glistening in the firelight, when frightened at the uproar and the change, the fish would again dart to the bottom, in fruitless efforts for freedom. . . .
>
> "This is a fearful expenditure of the choicest gifts of providence. These fish, Bess, which thou seest lying in such piles before thee . . . by tomorrow evening will be rejected food. . . .
>
> "But like all other treasures of the wilderness, they already begin to disappear, before the wasteful extravagance of man." (261–63)

• From Herman Melville's *Moby-Dick*, set during the first half of the nineteenth century, when fishing for whales was a major industry for New Englanders: Captain Ahab has charged the crew of his ship, the *Pequod*, with finding and destroying the whale that has maimed

Ahab. Here is the chief mate Starbuck's response to Ahab's an-
nouncement and Ahab's retort to Starbuck:

> "Vengeance on a dumb brute!" cried Starbuck, "that simply
> smote thee from blindest instinct! Madness! To be enraged
> with a dumb thing, Captain Ahab, seems blasphemous."
>
> "[The whale] tasks me; he heaps me; I see in him outra-
> geous strength, with an inscrutable malice sinewing it. That
> inscrutable thing is chiefly what I hate; and be the white whale
> agent, or be the white whale principal, I will wreak hate upon
> him. Talk not to me of blasphemy, man; I'd strike the sun if
> it insulted me." (139)

12. Create a dialogue between Santiago and another fisherman from his
    village to occur the day after Santiago returns to shore. Allow Santi-
    ago to recount the events at sea. Using information on marine or-
    ganisms from Dr. Kelley's interview, allow the other fisherman to
    respond, counter, or argue—as it seems to you appropriate—with
    what he would know about the marine organisms, including the mar-
    lin and the sharks, that Santiago encountered.

13. Reexamine the point of view from which *The Old Man and the Sea*
    is told. Notice what the point-of-view character, Santiago, knows and
    when he knows it. Based upon what you have learned in this chapter
    about marine organisms, are Santiago's thoughts and perceptions
    plausible or not? Write an essay in which you argue for or against the
    plausibility of Santiago's knowledge in *The Old Man and the Sea*.

SUGGESTED READINGS AND WORKS CITED

Allen, Thomas B. *The Shark Almanac*. New York: Lyons Press, 1999.

Brenner, Gerry. *The Old Man and the Sea: Story of a Common Man*.
Twayne Masterwork Studies No. 89. New York: Twayne Publishers,
1991.

Butler, James N., et al. *Studies of Sargassum and the Sargassum Community*. Ferry Reach, Bermuda: Bermuda Biological Station, 1983.

Cooper, James Fenimore. *The Pioneers*. New York: Holt, Rinehart & Winston, 1967.

Diaz, Henry F., and Roger S. Pulwarty, eds. *Hurricanes: Climate and
Socioeconomic Impacts*. Berlin: Springer, 1997.

Glotfelty, Cheryll, and Harold Fromm. *The Ecocriticism Reader: Land-
marks in Literary Ecology*. Athens: University of Georgia Press,
1996.

Gotto, R. V. *Marine Animals: Partnerships and Other Associations*. New
York: American Elsevier Publishing, 1969.

Hemingway, Ernest. *By-Line: Ernest Hemingway* Ed. William White New York: Touchstone, 1967.

———. "The Great Blue River." *Holiday* 6:1 (July 1949): 60–63, 95–97. Reprint, *True* 35 (April 1955): 21–30; Ernest Hemingway, *By-Line: Ernest Hemingway*, ed. William White (New York: Touchstone, 1967), 403–16.

———. "Marlin Off Cuba." *American Big Game Fishing*, ed. Eugene Connett. (New York: Derrydale Press, 1935), 55–81.

———. "Marlin Off the Coast of Morro: A Cuban Letter." *Esquire* 1:1 (Autumn 1933): 8, 39, 97. Reprint, Ernest Hemingway, *By-Line: Ernest Hemingway*, ed. William White (New York: Touchstone, 1967), 137–43.

———. "On the Blue Water: A Gulf Stream Letter." *Esquire* 5:4 (April 1936): 21, 184–85.

———. "Out in the Stream: A Cuban Letter." *Esquire* 2:3 (August 1934): 19, 156, 158. Reprint, Ernest Hemingway, *By-Line: Ernest Hemingway*, ed. William White (New York: Touchstone, 1967), 172–78.

———. "There She Breaches! Or Moby Dick Off the Morro." *Esquire* 5:5 (May 1936): 35, 203–5. Reprint, Ernest Hemingway, *By-Line: Ernest Hemingway*, ed. William White (New York: Touchstone, 1967), 245–54.

LeBuff, Charles R. *The Loggerhead Turtle in the Eastern Gulf of Mexico*. Sanibel, FL: Caretta Research, 1990.

Löfgren, Lars. *Ocean Birds*. New York: Knopf, 1984.

Melville, Herman. *Moby-Dick*. Boston: Houghton Mifflin, 1956.

Moss, Sanford A. *Sharks: An Introduction for the Amateur Naturalist*. Englewood Cliffs, NJ: Prentice Hall, 1984.

Nelson, Bryan. *Seabirds: Their Biology and Ecology*. New York: A&W Publishers, 1979.

Pequegrat, Willis E., and Ferrer A. Chace Jr., eds. *Contributions on the Biology of the Gulf of Mexico*. Houston, TX: Gulf Publishing Co., 1971.

Perry, Richard. *Watching Sea Birds*. New York: Taplinger, 1975.

Presley, Robert F. *Plankton, Nekton, and Nightlight Collections (Pf Series) with Pertinent Data: Yucatan Straits, Florida Straits, and Offshore Florida Waters*. St. Petersburg, FL: Marine Research Laboratory, 1971.

Pritchard, Peter Charles Howard. *Encyclopedia of Turtles*. Neptune, NJ: T.F.H. Publications, 1979.

Sylvester, Bickford. "The Cuban Context of *The Old Man and the Sea*." In *Modern Critical Interpretations: The Old Man and the Sea*, ed. Harold Bloom. Philadelphia: Chelsea House, 1999. 165–84.

U.S. Minerals Management Service. *Islands of Life: A Teacher's Companion!* New Orleans, LA: Minerals Management Service, 1997.

Waller, Geoffrey, ed. *SeaLife: A Complete Guide to the Marine Environment*. Washington, DC: Smithsonian Institution Press, 1996.

Walls, Jerry G. *Fishes of the Northern Gulf of Mexico*. Neptune, NJ: T.F.H. Publications, 1975.

Watson, George Earl. *Seabirds of the Tropical Atlantic Ocean*. Washington, DC: Smithsonian Institution Press, 1966.

Winn, Howard E., and Bori L. Olla, eds. *Behavior of Marine Animals: Current Perspectives in Research*. New York: Plenum Press, 1972.

3

Cuban Historical, Political, and Economic Background

The action of *The Old Man and the Sea* does not hinge upon particular historical events, as is the case for some of Hemingway's other works, particularly those based upon his own direct contact with historical occurrences. But the novella reveals many facets of Cuban history, politics, and economics in the depiction of Santiago as a typical commercial fisherman in Cuba before Fidel Castro came to power on New Year's Day in 1959.

Commercial fishing for marlin in the Gulf of Mexico has always provided Cubans with a living and with sustenance. Men such as Anselmo Hernandez—a fisherman Hemingway knew, who lived in Cojimar and who claimed he was the actual model for Santiago—made their living from the seas and supplied their country with a source of food. Moreover, the marlin, shark, and dolphin in the waters surrounding Cuba provided the island's residents with a livelihood in yet another way, through the tourist industry. Cubans such as Gregorio Fuentes—who was the captain of Hemingway's pleasure boat, the *Pilar*, and who is also considered a source for the character of Santiago—conducted wealthy tourists on game-fishing excursions in the Gulf of Mexico and the Straits of Florida.

Cuba's lush climate and natural resources had historically attracted these tourists and American expatriates who exploited the island for their own profit or pleasure. Ernest Hemingway was one of this group. Hemingway described Cuba's appeal in "The Great Blue River," which appeared in 1949 in *Holiday*, a magazine whose audience of rich Americans might be enticed to visit the exotic locations depicted in its pages. Cockfights and gambling at the shooting club—activities that were illegal Stateside—were diversions readily available to Hemingway in Cuba. But Cuba's greatest appeal for Hemingway lay in the game fishing its coastal waters afforded.

The type of person who traveled to Cuba for these recreations is represented on the last two pages of *The Old Man and the Sea* by the tourists at the Terrace who ask the waiter about the carcass of the marlin. The waiter responds with one word, "Tiburon," which he then attempts to translate for the tourists into English as "Eshark," in an effort to explain that the marlin had been ravaged by sharks. The tourists misunderstand, however, thinking that the carcass is that of a shark, a misunderstanding that signals the tourists' complete inability to comprehend what the native person knows about and experiences of Cuba. Indeed, the average Cuban, such as Santiago, shared little with these tourists to his island homeland, which, for him, was a place not of recreation, but of hard work, abject poverty, and social injustice. We can understand these circumstances of Santiago's life more fully when we know about the historical, political, and economic forces that shaped the life of an average Cuban fisherman during the period of Hemingway's writing of *The Old Man and the Sea*.

Christopher Columbus brought Spanish rule to Cuba in the late fifteenth century, and the indigenous people were soon rendered almost extinct because of the brutal treatment by the Spaniards, who then turned to Africa and the slave trade in order to supply the workforce for sugar plantations. At various points during the next three centuries, Cubans attempted to free themselves from Spanish rule. But notwithstanding Cuba's political and social problems, Americans flocked to the island during the nineteenth century for health and recreation, ignoring racial and class inequities in order to enjoy the pleasures the island offered. In 1868, Carlos Manuel de Céspedes led the Ten Year's War for Cuban independence, which culminated in a truce with Spain. Although still under Spanish rule, Cuba abolished slavery in 1886. In 1895, José Martí and General Máximo Gómez resumed the Cuban revolution, this time obtaining U.S. intervention.

At this time in Cuban history, the U.S. battleship *Maine* was docked in Havana harbor for the purpose of protecting the lives and property of American citizens in Cuba. On the morning of 15 February 1898, the *Maine* was blown up. Although the actual source of the explosion was not known, the Spanish were blamed, and the United States entered into a war against Spain. The treaty that ended the Spanish-American War in 1898 called for Spain to relinquish its rule over Cuba. The United States, however, maintained a military government there until 1902, when General Tomás Estrada Palma assumed the presidency of the Cuban Republic. But the United States continued its control through the Platt Amendment, passed in 1901. Drafted by Senator Orville Hitchcock Platt of Connecticut, this amendment to the U.S. Army Appropriations Bill stipulated conditions under which the United States could intervene in Cuban affairs. The unstable, conservative Palma government experienced several insurrections during its first years, and the United States, under the Platt Amendment, dispatched troops and took control of Cuba until 1909.

Throughout the first half of twentieth century, Cuba was a site of political turmoil and economic tension. The gap between the wealthy upper class and the impoverished lower class caused persistent political instability. Cuba continued, nonetheless, to be a recreational haven for North Americans. Cuba entered World War I on the side of the Allied forces, after which the United States continued its politics of intervention. In 1925, Gerardo Machado assumed the presidency of Cuba as a Liberal Party leader promising political reform, but eventually Machado functioned as a dictator before being forced out of the country in 1933. Cuba's internal political strife did not deter American tourists, however. In fact, during the Machado regime, Hemingway began to make regular trips to Cuba. While living in the Florida Keys and when lacking the privacy so necessary to his writing, Hemingway could travel quickly and easily to Cuba. He would rent a room at the Ambos Mundos Hotel (the name of this hotel translates, appropriately, to "both worlds") in Havana and frequent the Floridita, a somewhat shabby but always welcoming bar at which Hemingway became a regular for almost three decades. Hemingway was also drawn to Cuba because of the possibilities for fishing, and he caught his first big fish in Cuban waters during the summer of 1933. This success in fishing spurred Hemingway to take up journalism once more, now as a writer of articles on fishing and hunting for *Esquire* magazine.

The Platt Amendment was abrogated in 1934, furthering Cuba's independence from external rule. The 1930s witnessed Fulgencio Batista's control of the Senate; in 1940, Batista ascended to the presidency and was seen as a welcome change. Coming from humble roots, Batista had earned an education and military rank, and he promised to bring "law and order" to his country. During this (Batista's first) term as president of Cuba, which lasted through 1944, he oversaw both the establishment of a new Constitution and the country's entry in World War II against Germany, Japan, and Italy.

During World War II, Hemingway was living in Cuba at Finca Vigía (Lookout Farm), a villa in San Francisco de Paula that he had been able to purchase in December 1940. In 1942, eager as ever to be a participant in as well as a reporter of historical events, as he had been during World War I and the Spanish Civil War, Hemingway assembled a group of men dubbed the "Crook Factory" to ferret out pro-Nazi sources in Cuba. The group was headquartered at Finca Vigía and used a wide variety of informants—from priests to pimps to professional athletes to local fishermen. Hemingway's knowledge of the Spanish language enabled him to translate and process reports that he brought to the U.S. embassy in Havana. Hemingway then heeded the call to private citizens to patrol the Gulf of Mexico and the Straits of Florida, using his fishing boat, the *Pilar*, to scout for Nazi activity. In May 1942, Hemingway began his counterintelligence operation in Cuba, conducting his first shore patrol off the northwest coast of Cuba in July of that year. These patrols continued throughout 1943 and were finally discontinued in February 1944.

That year, Batista left office following the election of Ramón Grau San Martín, who himself was succeeded by the election of Carlos Prio Socarrás in 1948. During these relatively stable years in Cuban politics, Finca Vigía constituted Hemingway's principal residence. About twenty minutes from the city of Havana and ten miles from the sea, Finca Vigía enabled Hemingway to enjoy the glamour of the nearby city, the opportunities for deep-sea fishing, and the fraternity of local fishermen. In Havana, Hemingway and his guests could observe the nightlife and gambling that drew so many vacationing Americans to the island. The *Pilar*, now retired from surveillance duty, resumed its function as a vessel dedicated to fishing and other forms of maritime pleasure.

Fulgencio Batista once again took control of Cuba through a military coup in March 1952, but Batista, who gained power with the promise of law and order in the 1930s, had evolved into a dictator whose regime in the 1950s was characterized by a sharp division between the country's haves and have-nots. Shortly after Batista's second ascendancy to power, *Life* magazine printed *The Old Man and the Sea* in its 1 September edition, which was followed by the hardback published by Charles Scribner's Sons on 8 September. Santiago is drawn from the class of impoverished Cuban fishermen whom Hemingway had known for two decades, but *The Old Man and the Sea* did not articulate an explicit social agenda, nor did it argue for the reform of conditions that forced poor fishermen to live in abject poverty. Hemingway had long, and uncritically, enjoyed his position in Cuba as an affluent American who respected the skill of the professional Cuban fishermen and employed them in his own pursuit of pleasure through game fishing, but neither in life nor in fiction did he actively or explicitly attempt to better their economic conditions.

Nonetheless, *The Old Man and the Sea* was regarded worldwide as a work that presented the plight of the working class with enormous empathy. The novella prompted the Cuban government to honor Hemingway with three separate awards. On 23 September 1952, the Cuban Tourist Institute presented Hemingway the Medal of Honor, which he accepted "in the name of all commercial fishermen of the north coast of Cuba" ("Hemingway Gets Medal" 1). Two years later, on 21 July 1954, Batista conferred upon Hemingway the highest award granted to a civilian, the Order of Carlos Manuel de Céspedes, an award presented to "those who have worked for the progress of mankind and to forward the interests of Cuba" ("Cuba Honors Hemingway" 3). That Batista conferred this award was not without irony: An award created in honor of a Cuban leader (Céspedes) who had sought to liberate his people from oppressive rule was given by a Cuban leader (Batista) who, at this point in his history, had begun to oppress his people with a dictatorship (Reynolds 281). And on 17 November 1955, Hemingway received from the Cuban government the Order of San Cristóbal (Reynolds 291).

Hemingway also received international recognition for this no-

vella. The appeal of this book to the working class was acknowl-
edged when Italy's itinerant book peddlers awarded it their 1953
Barrow Prix as "the book of the year among the poor and middle
class persons who buy their reading matter from the barrow book-
stalls" ("Honor Without Profit" 3). That same year, *The Old Man
and the Sea* earned Hemingway the prestigious Pulitzer Prize in
literature; the novella was judged "the most distinguished fiction
published in book form during the year by an American author,
preferably dealing with American life," as reported in a *New York
Times* article. This same article explains that "The Cuban background of this prize winner is 'American' in the sense that the
other twenty republics of the Western Hemisphere are American,
too" (Bracker 24).

The Old Man and the Sea reclaimed for Hemingway his position
as one of the world's foremost men of literature at exactly the
moment that the plight of impoverished Cubans had become the
battle cry of a young lawyer named Fidel Castro, who would capture the world's attention for the remainder of the twentieth century and into the twenty-first. Born in 1927, Castro completed his
law degree at the University of Havana in 1950 and soon became
the leader of the movement to overthrow Batista. In 1953, Castro
led an unsuccessful uprising against Batista, after which he was
imprisoned on the Isle of Pines. There he wrote *History Will Absolve Me!* documenting his observations of conditions during the
early 1950s that had prompted him to lead the revolt. Released
from prison, Castro again attempted to overthrow Batista's government in 1956; again Castro was unsuccessful, but he fled to the
mountains of Cuba, whence he persisted in his assaults, using
guerrilla tactics, until his successful ouster of Batista on 1 January
1959.

The following excerpts and documents provide the reader with
an understanding of the ways in which the sociopolitical and economic situation in pre-Castro Cuba emerges as setting and influences character in *The Old Man and the Sea*. Through this
material, the reader can assess *The Old Man and the Sea* in the
context of information on commercial fishing and the living conditions of the typical Cuban fisherman as dictated by his class. Both
travel writers and politicians described conditions in Cuba but for
very different purposes. For the tourists like those at the end of
the novella, Cuba was an island of enchanted pleasure; they rarely

saw or understood the Cuba of Santiago, the one chronicled with such passionate vehemence by Fidel Castro. The excerpts that follow demonstrate these contrasting perceptions and explain the reception of *The Old Man and the Sea* as a text that deserved accolades for representing to the world the plight of the lower-class Cuban.

CUBA'S SOCIOECONOMIC AND POLITICAL SYSTEM AS CONTEXT FOR SANTIAGO'S LIFE

HEALTH AND WELL-BEING: AN EXAMINATION OF SANTIAGO AND OF MEDICAL FACTS

In *The Old Man and the Sea*, Santiago must deal with an immediate lack of food, water, and sleep, but these are deprivations that he has habitually experienced, deprivations associated with the class of persons to which Santiago belongs. His diet, his constant exposure to the elements, his fatigue, and the stress to his body caused by relentless, strenuous work, as well as the remedies he uses for his ailments, all bespeak the situation of the lower-class Cuban during the period of the novella's composition.

Dr. Arlyn Moeller, a physician who treats geriatric patients and who has extensive experience sailing in the Caribbean and the Gulf of Mexico, read *The Old Man and the Sea* and analyzed Santiago from the standpoint of a physician examining a patient. The interview with him that follows, therefore, focuses on the physical condition of an elderly, impoverished fisherman who exposes himself to the rigors of a three-day ordeal at sea. Dr. Moeller explains how numerous details from the text, such as Santiago's dizziness and nausea, are the biophysical consequences of dehydration, which is itself a consequence of his lack of fluid and days of exposure at sea. Notice how frequently Santiago's poverty is a key factor in his overall health and condition.

Dr. Moeller's examination of Santiago also suggests an alternative to the interpretation of "fakery" alleged by Robert P. Weeks, as explained in the previous chapter. Santiago's capacity to function during his three-day ordeal at sea is a feat that Weeks calls into question, using as evidence Hemingway's own account of a Cuban fisherman. Could someone like Santiago possess the physical capacity to endure as he did? Or, to frame this question within the historical and economic conditions facing a fisherman in Cuba in the late 1940s and early 1950s, could someone lacking both good nutrition and medical attention, facts implied by Santiago's poverty, have the stamina to not only survive three days at sea with very little water and food, but also fight a battle with a 1,500-pound marlin and assorted sharks? To answer this question, consider the evidence presented by Dr. Moeller.

INTERVIEW WITH DR. ARLYN MOELLER

(4 May 2000)

PV: Give us some insights into Santiago's physical condition and the probability that he could actually have endured and accomplished what he did, given the specific elements that are presented to us. On the very first page of the novella, we're told that Santiago has a skin cancer. He has what Hemingway describes as "brown blotches of the benevolent skin cancer the sun brings."

AM: Skin cancer was probably extremely frequent for people who sat out all day long fishing. They actually rode a skiff, and so they were essentially in the sun most of the time. This man, considered to be an old man, would probably have this kind of skin. It validated the type of [poor] person we're discussing.

PV: What kind of skin cancer would this be?

AM: Most likely either a basal cell or squamous cell carcinoma but not a malignant melanoma. Hemingway describes it as being dark. But if it was truly dark, it could be a melanoma, and then that would be metastatic; Santiago would have marked other physical conditions. My guess is, because Hemingway says it's the type that happens to people who are in the sun, that probably either [it] was a basal cell or squamous cell carcinoma. That's mainly local.

PV: Next question has to do with the apparent lack of nutrition that this man has.

AM: By any standard that we [twenty-first-century Americans] would have of a balanced diet, he had an absolutely poor diet.

PV: He gets a meal of black beans, rice, fried bananas, and stew that the boy brings him from the restaurant the night before he goes out. But the morning that he departs from land—which would occur the second day of the novella—he drinks coffee, and the narrator says that Santiago knows that it will be all that he [has] for the day. So he proposes to go out in his boat after only a cup of coffee for the morning.

AM: He was planning on being out there for only one day. He didn't expect what happened to him.

PV: Exactly. Would it be reasonable for a person in this situation to assume that he would have the stamina to function for a day without having eaten anything, with just a cup of coffee?

AM: What the boy had brought to him, that was unusual because that's not the way he normally ate. He normally was very fatigued and would just eat whatever he could capture. The boy brought him more food and a balanced diet, but that was one meal [and] that's not the way the man normally ate.

PV: Santiago said he had a habit of drinking a cup of shark liver oil every day. Do you know anything about that?

AM: Yes. It contains vitamin D. In the United States for years, cod liver oil [had been used. In Cuba,] there was shark liver oil, but it's the same thing. It's relatively nutritious and ugly tasting. It would not compensate for the fact that he had such a poor diet otherwise. Taking as much as he had is kind of amazing. And I would also imagine that if you drank a cup, it would act as a laxative.

PV: It's interesting you mention the laxative because on a number of occasions he mentions nausea and diarrhea. Maybe he shouldn't have been drinking all that shark oil! At the end of the first day, Santiago drinks a little bit of water, and that's the only time he talks about urinating of the side of the boat. But I don't find many other sections of the novella—until he gets back to shore—when he mentions drinking water. If a person were floating around at sea for a day like that, with so little water, what would happen? Multiply this out by three more days. What would happen to a person that age with so little water?

AM: It was a hot day, the sun was bright, he was down in the Gulf of Mexico, where the sun is very intense, of course. You can't drink seawater because it's salt water. In twenty-four hours, in that exposure, where there's very little water, a person would normally already be having the symptoms of dehydration.

PV: And what are they?

AM: They would be [symptoms] which Hemingway brings up: dizziness, weakness, delirium, confusion, hallucinations. . . . This . . . has a lot to do with Santiago's dehydration, and from a nutritional standpoint, he was already malnourished.

PV: Yes, and that brings us to his food. By the end of the first day, he's caught a tuna that he then uses for bait, but he thinks about the fact that he has to eat the tuna. It's not that he has an appetite and thinks, "Oh, I'm so hungry; when can I eat?" He bears in mind that he better eat the tuna the next day because it'll go bad. What about this lack of appetite?

AM: First of all, the man has been, apparently, used to living on very little food. He eats the tuna, and this is basically just eating some protein. The tuna doesn't have any carbohydrates. And he took it because he knew that he needed some sort of nutrition, but his nutrition is unbalanced because he only takes what he can have available.

PV: Does the depression of his appetite have to do with the fact that his body is accustomed to eating so little food?

AM: Yes, and the depression of his appetite also has to do with the fact that he's dehydrated and feels very weak. And when people become weak, they become anorexic—that is, they lack appetite.

PV: His hand starts to cramp at the beginning of the second day.

AM: It's because of electrolyte imbalance.

PV: Could you explain that?

AM: He probably has an imbalance of his salt in his blood because he has been sweating in the sun and not taking any electrolytes or any salts back in. His potassium is going down, and he's getting muscle spasm from a combination of dehydration and electrolyte imbalance.

PV: And this would be something that anybody under those circumstances might experience?

AM: Yes, but especially with Santiago, because he probably didn't start out with a normal electrolyte profile because of his dietary habits.

PV: Very interesting. Santiago realizes that he can't open his left hand because it's so badly cramped. Then he thinks that probably after he's eaten the tuna and digested it, the hand will open. Is that a medically sound opinion?

AM: Yes, and it suggests that he's had some experience with muscle spasm in the past. This is not his first experience with being out at sea for quite a long time, in the hot sun, with poor nutrition, and poor fluids, and . . . if he gets food, fluid, and nutrition, the muscle spasm will abate. . . .

PV: So the symptoms and treatment that Santiago experiences have some foundation in biophysical reality?

AM: Yes. When patients are having muscle spasm, we do [an] electrolyte profile, and if potassium's low, we give them either oral or I.V. potassium, and it relieves the spasm very promptly.

PV: I did not know that about muscle spasms. A muscle spasm is the same thing as cramps?

AM: Yes. Most of the people complain more [about cramps] in their legs, but . . . [h]e's sitting in a boat. He's using his arms because that's what he's using to fish with. He's not walking. Women or men that have low potassium usually complain about leg cramps because that's what they use the most. But for him, he's sitting in a boat. He's not using his muscles in his legs.

PV: So the muscles that are used the most are going to have the spasm when they're starved for potassium. Let's turn now to the subject of Santiago's fatigue or sleep deprivation. The end of the second day, he starts realizing that he needs sleep. What would a person be like if he were floating about at sea, in the hot sun, dehydrated and malnourished, with no sleep?

AM: Lack of sleep exacerbates all other psychological problems. Adding sleep deprivation to his other problems of dehydration and electrolyte imbalance contributes to the continual narrowing of his thought process.

PV: So the narrowing of the thought process is consistent with all other physical challenges. Depriving people food, water, and sleep causes the thought process to become more focused?

AM: True, they eventually become hallucinatory; but for healthy, well-nourished people, it would take longer than for those who didn't start out healthy.

PV: Santiago says that he's going to eat some of the dolphin which he has caught. That's raw. He says he wishes that he had salt or water with him because he's very much afraid at this point of becoming nauseous.

AM: And nausea, of course, is part of dehydration, and Santiago knows that. I think that he knows that he's weak, and consequently he feels like his body is not going to be able to do a good job of tolerating oral foods. When people get dehydrated enough, they have to have I.V. fluids because they can't stop vomiting until they get fluids back in. The same thing [happens when] they get I.V. fluids for diarrhea; it will stop because they get their electrolyte balance back to normal because they lose sodium chloride by vomiting, and they lose potassium through their stool.

PV: The fishing line moving through Santiago's hand starts to cause his right hand to bleed, and he puts his hand in the water to get salt water?

AM: Sure. We do saline soaks for people who have lacerated hands or infected hands. We use saline, and saline has the same consistency of salt as seawater. It heals and soothes irritated skin and lesions, and that's why he soaks it.

PV: When he starts eating other fish, raw flying fish, one of the things he is continuously worried about is being nauseous. In fact, he talks about how it's so embarrassing to have ptomaine poisoning and be nauseous or to have diarrhea. But he says at this point it's better to be light-headed—that is, from hunger—than to be nauseous from eating the raw fish, which is too unpalatable. Now, that's an unpleasant set of choices.

AM: Some of the fish that he had doesn't taste as good raw as others do. He was having a hard time consuming anything, and so that made him even more selective. And he was wishing that he had salt to make it more palatable.

PV: And at the beginning of the third day at sea, which is the fourth day of the story, he starts to see black spots before his eyes.

AM: A visual lack is very common because of a dropping blood pressure when you're dehydrated.

PV: Oh, so those black spots come from low blood pressure?

AM: Black spots and decreased vision are very typical of dehydration, related to the fact that in dehydration, you have low blood volume, low circulating volume, so consequently you have a drop in your blood pressure.

PV: Now explain what you mean by low circulating volume.

AM: Your blood volume is reduced because you're talking about reduced fluid; there's not enough [fluid] circulating, and so your blood pressure drops.

PV: Santiago attributes the spots before his eyes to the level of tension he's exerting on the line that he's pulling.

AM: If you exert effort, and your blood pressure is marginal, and you're weak and almost ready to faint, I think pulling in the line would enhance the symptomology. . . . He was perspiring a lot and losing a lot of salt through his perspiration, and I was wondering if he was actually concerned about the possibility, with all the stress, of falling out of the boat because he was so weak.

PV: Yes. At this point, he says he's more tired than he's ever been, but in this condition at the end of the third day, he finally reels the fish in, and, according to his calculations, it's supposed to be 1,500 pounds! Now, Arlyn, is there any way that an old man in this physical condition could do this?

AM: This fish came to him. It had to have done that.

PV: He couldn't, he couldn't have reeled the fish to the boat.

AM: No, no.

PV: There's no way.

AM: But the fish was tied to the boat, and that's why the boat was traveling, you know, because the fish was pulling the boat. The fish pulled the boat to sea. Now the boat is a strain on the fish. We've talked about the physical stress on Santiago, but we can't forget about the physical stress on the fish. Santiago wore the fish out. That was Santiago's purpose until the fish finally would come up, and that's what happened after three days when the fish finally came to him. He didn't go to the fish.

PV: When the sharks start to attack, Santiago exerts himself in perhaps ways greater than even getting the marlin lashed to the boat because he uses his harpoon, and he's fighting them off.

AM: He's angry.

PV: Can a person who hasn't eaten—or who has eaten only a little raw fish—is it possible for somebody who has been fending off nausea and dizziness and black spots before his eyes and, to the best of our knowledge, has had only some water during this three-day ordeal, can a person do what Hemingway describes Santiago doing?

AM: I think that what Santiago's doing is an effort, . . . and I think [he uses] everything that he's got left.

PV: Could an old man who's malnourished, who didn't have any help, who didn't have any shade, he didn't have much water, could he physically be capable of doing this, or would you say by this time he would have passed out?

AM: Well, I think that he could stay with the activity, but I don't think he was doing very much. I think that every single thing he did was probably the max [effort for] what he tried. He took this oar and tried to battle the shark. These were sporadic, momentary efforts on his part, but I don't think that he had continuous activity. He was seeing the problem, he was trying to address the problem, he was angry and upset, and the sharks were taking away what he had worked so hard for, so there was an adrenaline thrust for momentary issues only, and then he backed off.

PV: At the end of the third night, he is stiff and sore and cold and hurting. He arrives at shore, and he gets back to his shack. On the morning of the fifth day, the boy comes and brings him coffee. He says he's going to go out and get him some other food. How would you characterize his physical condition at this point?

AM: The fellow was obviously extremely exhausted. He had been sleep deprived, he was a weakened fellow to begin with, and he was certainly dehydrated. He got into the bed because there was nothing else in the world that he could do for himself because he was at the end of his endurance. And so consequently, when he got home, he only thought about lying down.

PV: Now, if you had a person like this, you probably would have put him on an I.V., wouldn't you?

AM: Oh, I would certainly do that.

POVERTY AND OPPRESSION OF LOWER-CLASS CUBANS

The excerpts from the following publications present the plight of the poor Cuban from two separate perspectives. Excerpts from the piece titled "The Island Next Door" present an American's report on numerous indicators of Cuban poverty: substandard housing, crowding, lack of medical attention, poor sanitation. Such conditions created a fertile breeding ground for revolutionary insurgents such as Fidel Castro, excerpts from whose writings comprise the second selection. Jailed after his failed attempt to overthrow Batista in what came to be known as the "26th July Movement" of 1953, Castro wrote *La Historia Me Absolverá*, or as it is translated into English, *History Will Absolve Me* as his defense plea, delivered before the Emergency Tribunal of Santiago de Cuba on 16 October 1953. This text presents Castro's impassioned statement on the conditions facing poor Cubans during the early 1950s. In the excerpts below, Castro describes the poverty of his nation's citizens, invoking the name and inspiration of an earlier revolutionary, José Martí. Amid high rhetoric in what is clearly a propaganda document, Castro cites infant mortality and disease, substandard housing, and a mismanaged economic system as the reasons for the island's poverty and the reasons why he believes he can count upon its citizens to join his revolution.

FROM HELEN HALL, "THE ISLAND NEXT DOOR"

(*Survey Graphic* 24 [February 1935])

In contrast, the "shanty-towns," as with us, represent what landless and workless people have done for themselves. Characteristically enough, they are built of Cuba's waste, of the boots of palm trees that have been used as wrapping for tobacco bales, but they look like our "shanty-towns" in the United States put together these last five years from tin cans and packing boxes. These small settlements are often referred to as *llega-y-pon* which, translated, means "arrive and flop." There is, however, a great deal more to it than the name suggests, for these small villages have persisted and spread, and the pattern of community life soon asserts itself. Paths become little streets with names and the houses have their numbers. Tiny shacks appear as grocery stores displaying a few cans and tobacco and a few bananas. Even the distinction of rich and poor has its expression, for at the end of one town we came upon a particularly miserable hut where a black baby was being fed some yellow cornmeal. "That is the hut of a poor woman," said the so-called mayor. "She is too poor to build a better house. This," he explained, "just keeps off the rain." The mayor was himself ragged enough and so were his citizens but some of the women wore earrings and necklaces which were reassuring evidence of what never dies. And there were huts which revealed a sense of artistry and had an air of well-being, even in the heat and squalor of their surroundings—striking examples of the way people reach out for the benefits and decencies of civilization in spite of every obstacle. Yet in their lack of sanitation, of education, of any scheme for bringing the social resources of the community to bear on life, these villages illustrated, in an extreme form, needs that we found repeated in the small towns of Cuba and in outlying country districts. (74)

• • •

Cuba and the United States are in truth two of the most backward of the civilized nations in developing housing for working people. While very little has as yet been done in Havana, in the small towns the need is even greater. Here there is not the old architecture of the cities, nor the quaint thatched roofs of the country-sides to relieve the squalor. Built sometimes of stucco, sometimes of wood, small houses along streets often scarcely passable for mud present pitiable living conditions both inside and out. Indoors, in the poorer districts of the towns, one finds little more than is essential to life. The inevitable rusty spring beds without mattresses seemed a tragic overture of our mechanical civilization to people it had not otherwise benefited. Mud floors are frequent and very often the families have no gardens. They live huddled together getting the benefits neither of city nor country.

Look for a moment at a composite picture of four towns visited which may be considered a fair cross-section of adverse conditions, as two of them were in the older settled portions of the island, one in the cattle country, with cowboys driving a herd through the streets and the fourth, a one-street town, built up from the mud at a railway junction in the newer cane country to the East. For range, one had 12,000 inhabitants, another 4000, a third 2000 and the fourth 500. Only in the larger communities was there water supply, the smallest depending on rain water; and neither water nor sewage reached to the poorer streets anywhere. The one hospital in the largest town, with a budget for twenty patients, attempted to care for forty. There were no hospital facilities in the other towns; in one, no doctor at all. The schools were less adequate than in city districts; the most meager accommodations being in the smallest town, its one room open three months in the year, with fifty children enrolled and sixty-five unprovided for as shown by a recent canvass. (76–77)

FROM FIDEL CASTRO, *HISTORY WILL ABSOLVE ME*

(New York: Center for Cuban Studies, 1953)

When we speak of struggle and we mention the people we mean the vast unredeemed masses, those to whom everyone makes promises and who are deceived by all; we mean the people who yearn for a better, more dignified and more just nation; who are moved by ancestral aspirations of justice, for they have suffered injustice and mockery generation after generation; those who long for great and wise changes in all aspects of their life; people who, to attain those changes, are ready to give even the very last breath they have, when they believe in something or in someone, especially when they believe in themselves. The first condition of sincerity and good faith in any endeavor is to do precisely what nobody else ever does, that is, to speak with absolute clarity, without fear. The demagogues and professional politicians who manage to perform the miracle of being right about everything and of pleasing everyone are, necessarily, deceiving everyone about everything. The revolutionaries must proclaim their ideas courageously, define their principles and express their intentions so that no one is deceived, neither friend nor foe.

In terms of struggle, when we talk about people we're talking about the *six hundred thousand* Cubans without work, who want to earn their daily bread honestly without having to emigrate from their homeland in search of a livelihood; the *five hundred thousand* farm laborers who live in miserable shacks, who work four months of the year and starve the rest.

• • •

Just as serious or even worse is the housing problem. There are *two hundred thousand* huts and hovels in Cuba; *four hundred thousand families* in the countryside and in the cities live cramped in huts and tenements without even the minimum sanitary requirements; *two million two hundred thousand* of our urban population pay rents which absorb between one fifth and one third of their incomes; and *two million eight hundred thousand* of our rural and suburban population lack electricity. We have the same situation here: if the State proposes the lowering of rents, landlords threaten to freeze all construction; if the State does not interfere, construction goes on so long as the landlords get high rents; otherwise they would not lay a single brick even though the rest of the population had to live totally exposed to the elements. The utilities monopoly is no better; they extend lines as far as it is profitable and beyond that point they don't care if people have to live in darkness for the rest of their lives. The State sits back with its arms crossed and the people have neither homes nor electricity.

Our educational system is perfectly compatible with everything I've just mentioned. Where the peasant doesn't own the land, what need is there for agricultural schools? Where there is no industry, what need is there for technological or vocational schools? Everything follows the same absurd logic; if we don't have one thing we can't have the other. In any small European country there are more than 200 technological and vocational schools; in Cuba only six such schools exist, and the graduates have no jobs for their skills. The little rural schoolhouses are attended by a mere half of the school age children—barefooted, half-naked and undernourished—and frequently the teacher must buy necessary school materials from his own salary. Is this the way to make a nation great?

Only death can liberate one from so much misery. In this respect, however, the State is most helpful—in providing early death for the people. *Ninety percent* of the children in the countryside are consumed by parasites which filter through their bare feet from the ground they walk on. Society is moved to compassion when it hears of the kidnapping or murder of one child, but it is criminally indifferent to the mass murder of so many thousands of children who die every year from lack of facilities, agonizing with pain. Their innocent eyes, death already shining in them, seem to look into some vague infinity as if entreating forgiveness for human selfishness, as if asking God to stay wrath. And when the head of a family works only four months a year, with what can he purchase clothing and medicine for his children? They will grow up with rickets, with not a single good tooth in their mouths by the time they reach thirty; they will have heard ten million speeches and will finally die of misery and deception. Public hospitals, which are always full, accept only patients recommended by some powerful politician who, in turn, demands the electoral votes of the unfortunate one and his family so that Cuba may continue forever in the same or worse condition. (28–29)

• • •

Cuba could easily provide for a population three times as great as it has now, so there is no excuse for the abject poverty of a single one of its present inhabitants. The markets should be overflowing with produce, pantries should be full, all hands should be working. This is not an inconceivable thought. What is inconceivable is that anyone should go to bed hungry while there is a single inch of unproductive land; that children should die for lack of medical attention; what is inconceivable is that 30 percent of our farm people cannot write their names and that 99 percent of them know nothing of Cuba's history. What is inconceivable is that the majority of our rural people are now living in worse circumstances than the Indians Columbus discovered in the fairest land that human eyes had ever seen.

To those who would call me a dreamer, I quote the words of Martí: 'A true man does not seek the path where advantage lies, but rather the path where duty lies, and this is the only practical man, whose dream of today will be the law of tomorrow, because he who has looked back on the essential course of history and has seen flaming and bleeding peoples seethe in the cauldron of the ages, knows that, without a single exception, the future lies on the side of duty.' (32–33)

HOUSING FOR THE POOR CUBAN: THE PALM HUT

The excerpt below is from an article on Cuban life published in *Holiday* magazine. The author enthusiastically describes the lush foliage of the island. Moreover, Bemelmans's article explains that the palm is used to make huts for poor Cubans. Although the excerpt begins with comparisons of the Cuban landscape to depictions by famous painters of the late nineteenth and early twentieth centuries, the passage concludes with a blunt description of the poverty of homes in which humans and animals survive under one roof. The description of the palm hut, like that in Barbour's writing, demonstrates the use put to natural resources found in Cuba, but the excerpt below should also be compared with Castro's remarks about housing for his poor countrymen. Hemingway tells us that Santiago's hut is made of palm, but Santiago does not share his home with any other living thing.

FROM LUDWIG BEMELMANS, "THE BEST WAY TO SEE CUBA"

(*Holiday* 22 [1957])

There are landscapes of great beauty in Cuba, of soft Pissarro and Cézanne color, and the tropical intensity of Gauguin. Most leaves on trees are round, the needles of the pines are soft, and some trees bear blossoms that look like the plumage of birds of paradise. The fields of sugar cane are of a green which is richer than any other. The earth is a moist burnt sienna.

There are mountains, hills and valleys, the vegetation varies in intensity from dense jungle to cultivated land—sugar here, tobacco there, oranges, bananas, pineapple.

The most radiantly beautiful object in nature here is the royal palm, which stands straight, perfectly balanced. Its silvered-gray trunk, which rises house-high, endows the land with splendor as do the columns of temples in Greece. Other palm trees, notably the coconut palm, lean this way and that, and have a generally unkempt appearance.

The royal palm stands anywhere, is sometimes found in rows a kilometer long, lining the lane to a farmhouse. It also stands as in a forest, and it may be found beside the house of the poorest farmer. Farmer is a word that does not apply here, really, for he is in most cases a worker in the cane fields and in the sugar mills, which employ him for three months of the year.

He lives in a house called a *bohio*, which is entirely constructed of the royal palm tree. The outside of this tree is hard and is used for the walls; the fronds are used for the thatched roof. Pigs and chickens share the house, and the pigs are fed the fruit of the royal palm, a kind of date unfit for people. (228)

THE FISHING INDUSTRY IN CUBA AS SANTIAGO PARTICIPATED IN IT

Santiago's method of fishing for a living required enormous skill and endurance, but it was not a method calculated to reap an abundant food supply for Cuban citizens. The following article in *Americas* reprints in translation an editorial that had appeared in the Havana newspaper *Diario de la Marina*. The editor calls for

Cubans to recognize the potential for fishing in the surrounding seas. The article implies that the effort of an individual fisherman is not as cost-effective or as beneficial to Cuba's economy as it might be. Instead of contributing wealth to the Cuban economy, Santiago's method of commercial fishing explains the country's poverty.

FROM "WEALTH IN THE DEEP"

(*Americas* 5 [1953])

Cuba has long been trying to lessen its dependence on sugar, and the editors of Havana's *Diario de la Marina* are convinced that Old King Neptune holds one of the answers:

"The Ministry of Agriculture recently chose as the subject for the Alvaro Reynoso Journalistic Contest 'Fishing Opportunities in Cuba.' ... We want to take this opportunity to say that in our opinion it is high time Cuba gave more thought to nearby and distant waters as a source of wealth, employment, and protein-rich food for its citizens.

"We have to wake up to the fact that we are an island people and that therefore our economic development should begin with an intensive exploitation of our maritime fauna. It's time we stopped depending on foreign fishing industries to the tune of ten million pesos a year.

"We import an annual twelve thousand tons of codfish alone. Why doesn't Cuba organize its own fishing fleets to look for cod in the Newfoundland waters? European ships cross the Atlantic to get the fish, take it home for processing, and then send it to us across thousands of additional nautical miles. It seems incredible that Cuba has not taken advantage of being nearer to those rich fishing grounds to keep all those millions of pesos at home and open broad new fields for maritime and industrial employment.

"But right here in our own territorial waters we are surrounded by tremendous wealth, which is being exploited only casually and with techniques that are out of date. Some progress has been made in obtaining and preserving such products as bonito and lobster, but only on a small scale. For lack of the right equipment, we have to let the huge schools of migratory fish pass by, thus depriving Cubans of cheap, succulent food.

"In addition to streamlining fishing equipment, we need to expand our canneries and our facilities for rapid distribution. A huge packing house should be built in Havana, where fishing boats could deposit their take and go right back to sea the same day instead of waiting around in the bay for market prices to rise. This would mean that an adequate supply of fish would always be available at lower prices than prevail now, and the industry would be more stable from the point of view of both investors and workers.

"Another wide-open field is that of by-products, such as fertilizers and fish flour for feeding animals.

"We have in our country, besides favorable natural and geographic conditions, men of great skill in the arts and industries of the ocean, and plenty of available capital and labor. All we need, then, is the decision to use all these assets in a coordinated effort, a voice of authority to say to our maritime industry: 'Get up and walk.' Let's hope that the Ministry of Agriculture's contest will herald the long-awaited and happy day when we return to the sea." (35)

CUBA'S SOCIOECONOMIC AND POLITICAL SYSTEM AS CONTEXT FOR THE TOURISTS' EXPERIENCE

Cuba's socioeconomic and political system during the late 1940s and early 1950s accounted for Santiago's poverty, the circumstances of his housing, and his practice of commercial fishing. That same system of economics and politics sustained a tourist industry in Cuba that drew numerous Americans to its shores, such as those tourists introduced briefly at the end of the novella. These Americans had an experience of Cuba that was radically different from that of the average Cuban, represented by Santiago. Excerpts from the following articles explain the allure of Cuba for U.S. tourists. Cuba, readily accessible and very inexpensive for Americans, was an island of pleasures, some of which, such as gambling, were illegal almost everywhere in the United States during the late 1940s and 1950s. In addition to gambling and other forms of nightlife, Cuba's beautiful landscape and beaches provided Americans with the perfect getaway spot. But these Americans were largely ignorant of the reality of the average Cuban's experience, as is demonstrated by the tourists at the Terrace in *The Old Man and the Sea*. This couple completely misunderstands what their waiter is saying about the carcass of Santiago's marlin. The excerpts below indicate what the tourists would have known of Cuba and how they might pass their days during a Cuban vacation.

GAMBLING AND NIGHTLIFE FOR THE TOURIST IN CUBA

The excerpt below explains how Cuba's economy benefited from tourism. The writer for *Travel* magazine extolls the pleasures available to wealthy Americans through the "Fly by Night Club," so named on the basis of Pan American Airlines' nightly flights from Miami to Havana, which returned tourists to Florida at dawn after a night of gambling and entertainment in Cuban nightclubs. On page 71 of *The Old Man and the Sea*, Santiago notices an airplane in the sky en route to Miami.

FROM NINA WILCOX PUTNAM, "TO HAVANA WITH THE FLY BY NIGHT CLUB"

(*Travel* 90 [1947])

When you have been lounging all day on Miami Beach trying to recover from looking at your hotel bill, you can get away from it all by stepping into your room, into your evening clothes, into the plane, and very shortly thereafter be turned lose among the biggest variety of night clubs in the world. It is something like having a night on the tiles of pre-war Paris, but far less trouble. There is no bother with passports, luggage, customs, inspectors or foreign currency: in short, no headaches—unless you bring one back.

The Night Club Special wings its way from Miami's 36th Street airport every evening at eight, and lands you, seventy minutes later at the Raucho Boyeros, the *a la carte* name of the Havana field. Then by the dawn's early light, the same plane brings what is left of you back to Miami, leaving that brancho of the Rancho at 6 A.M.

From its maiden but scarcely maidenly first trip on November 9, 1946, the Special has been booked as solidly in advance as a Broadway hit show. So successful has Operation Rum and Rumba proven that just before last Christmas the Cuban National Casino, a government-sponsored gambling establishment which makes Monte Carlo look like a three-card Monte outfit, started up a Special of its own. This Flight of Fancy takes place at 7 P.M. on Saturday only, and is called, flatteringly, The Millionaire's Special. While the more democratic PAA [Pan Ameican Airlines] nightly-flighters must pay for their transportation, the Millionaire is for free. On it, the guests of the Casino are said to be served unlimited champagne and caviar—also without charge.

However, as with most free things there is a hook. Flight is by invitation only, and while these invitations are sent to a list of persons selected ostensibly because of their importance, which ranges from the High C of the social register to the depths of the newspaper columnist world, the names are popularly rumored to be taken from the secret archives of Miami's hush-hush plush gambling parlors. People who play the fifty cent tables never get an invite. But the thousand-dollar-bill boys are given a season-pass.

Almost every first-class night club in Havana has a licensed gambling room and the low class ones have plain gambling. . . .

Cuban taste is not like ours. We like our shows hot like coffee; they like 'em hot like Cayenne pepper. And Havana's night clubs are not only out of this country, they are out of this world. Many of them are also out in the open air.

The Tropicana is one of these which flourish in the shade of the out-stretched palm. Once a millionaire's home, the spacious rooms are too small to accommodate the patrons except for gambling in what was once the ball-room where reminders of past, more conservative glories are still visible. The actual night club is out in one of the finest of tropical gardens, where dozens of flower-laden tables slope toward a curiously shaped modernistic band-shell and a small dance-floor. From the entrance-steps it seems like a vision seen through the wrong end of a telescope. The vast place is more like a corral than a patio for size, but is well wired for sound.

The girls in the show shake the rumba to its very depths, and the Afro-Cuban entertainers might be very funny if only you understand Spanish. Could be very naughty, too. For here as in all Cuban night spots singers like the great Rita Montaner stick a hot innuendo into their songs and most of them could sing the alphabet in a way to make you blush! Possibly though, they can't help what's in your mind when they are merely vocalizing about how they love rice and chicken.

Newest of night clubs is the Montmartre, possibly so called after its famous namesake because it, too, overlooks the city. If there is another like it, I don't know where. The entire building was recently reconstructed at a cost of $200,000 to serve as luxury nest for the night-hawk. Located on the roof, with a superb view out over never-sleeping Havana, it has mirrored ceilings, an illuminated glass dance-floor. After tunnelling through the curvacious modernistic bar one emerges into the main room and pauses awe-stricken by the confronting nudes which stand, a good twenty feet tall, on either side of a fountain sending multi-colored jets of water toward the starlit heavens. Concrete is comparatively cheap and plentiful in Cuba and these naked ladies, huge and heavy of limb, are more likely to appeal to a Gauguin than to the average American who is still inclined to admire September Morn.

Everything else at the Montmartre is also super-duper, from the sound-proofed gaming-rooms provided with a silencer ceiling, presumably so you can't hear your last dollar crying for help. The lower section houses all the club's employees from M.C.s to busboys in luxurious rooms with private baths, even a garage for their cars, which, judging from the tips expected, must be new and many. The floor show is the most expensive that money can buy, a fact you can check when you get your check. . . .

However, the preponderance of night club performers are Cubans, usually Afro-Cubans, and the most popular number is the Rumba, which is not at all what you think it is.

The thing you dance if you and Arthur Murray claim you rumba, is really the *danzon*. No non-professional can, and no conservative lady would, dance the real rumba. And what's more, the *danzon* is not really the *danzon*, either, but an adaptation of the *son*, a frankly courting-dance still done in its indigenous form throughout Central America. In it the man and girl dance opposite each other without clinching, the two of them hopping around with birdlike steps. African cranes, wrens, and even ostriches dance the *son*, the ostrich later hiding his head so as not to see what he's got himself into. The *danzon* is a streamlined version of the *son*. But the rumba, the real McCoy, is a dance-drama with a plot about boy gets girl, and in Cuba you clearly realize this from the start.

A good example of this *pièce sans resistance* can probably be found at the Zombie, in mid town Havana not far from Sloppy Joe's, which may or may not be the original home of the drink Ma told you never to touch, but even if you obey her you will still be knocked out by the Rumba of the Rose. The photo-finish is furnished when the boy, in the middle of a handspring, without using anything but his mouth, snatches a rose from between the lips of the wiggling girl who is flat on the floor. (17–19)

TOPICS FOR WRITTEN OR ORAL EXPLORATION

1. Read Hemingway's other fictional works set in Cuba, *Islands in the Stream* and *To Have and Have Not*, and write an essay in which you compare and contrast specific elements of setting drawn from Cuban history and politics. In your conclusion, argue which works incorporate Cuban history and politics more specifically and why.

2. Robert P. Weeks asserts that Hemingway knew that an old fisherman could not perform Santiago's feat *and* retain his composure and sanity—a key factor in Santiago's characterization and the novella's plot. Using evidence from the interview with Dr. Moeller, refute Weeks's contention with specific facts based upon biophysical information.

3. Read Hemingway's articles about Cuba and the waters surrounding it that he wrote for various periodicals. Write an essay in which you describe the facets of Cuba that Hemingway experienced. How is the Cuba of Hemingway's experience similar to or different from the Cuba that is depicted in *The Old Man and the Sea*?

4. Read the newspaper reports of awards earned by *The Old Man and the Sea* and, using information from these articles as well as relevant excerpts provided above, write an essay in which you argue that the novella deserves its awards for portraying the life of the workingman in Cuba. Discuss the extent to which the depiction of Cuba's socioeconomic situation might have contributed to the novella's stature in the eyes of the public.

5. Pretend you are one of the tourists at the end of *The Old Man and the Sea*. Write either a journal entry or a letter from the perspective of the male or the female tourist in which you record several days' activities during that person's Cuban vacation.

6. Write a letter to one of the tourists in *The Old Man and the Sea*. Explain to that person at least five aspects of Santiago's experience in Cuba that differ from the tourist's.

7. Assess Hemingway's articles about Cuba and the waters surrounding it from the perspective of a Cuban fisherman such as Santiago and the two tourists at the end of the novella. Do Hemingway's descriptions and his experiences more closely match the experiences of the Cuban fisherman or the tourists to Cuba?

8. Refer to the interview with Dr. Moeller and make a list of Santiago's medical or health conditions and treatment (or lack of treatment) for these conditions. How many items on this list imply Santiago's poverty? Make an oral report to your class in which you present this list and your rationale behind identifying the items on it as demonstrations of Santiago's poverty.

9. Santiago seems entirely resigned to his situation. "Resignation" is hardly a word that would describe Fidel Castro's response to the circumstances of poverty in Cuba. Create a dialogue between Castro and Santiago in which the two men discuss the socioeconomic situation of their lives in Cuba. What would be the tone of this dialogue? Argumentative? Persuasive? Sympathetic? Could the dialogue conclude with one man convincing the other of the value of his position, with the two men finding common ground?

10. Compare and contrast the tone of Bemelmans's piece with the tone of Castro's writing. Each man mentions Cuban housing, but how do they differ in their discussion of the huts in which many Cubans live? Whose tone is closer to the one used to describe Santiago's hut in *The Old Man and the Sea*? What does Hemingway's tone suggest about the position on poverty in Cuba taken in the novella?

SUGGESTED READINGS AND WORKS CITED

Bracker, Milton. "1953 Pulitzer Prize Won by Hemingway and 'Picnic.' " *New York Times*, 5 May 1953 1:2, 24.

"Cuba Honors Hemingway: Highest Award for a Foreigner Is Pinned on Author." *New York Times*, 22 July 1954, 3:3.

Foner, Philip S. *A History of Cuba and Its Relations with the United States*, Vol. I, *1492–1845*. New York: International Publishers, 1962.

Fuentes, Norberto. *Ernest Hemingway Rediscovered*. New York: Charles Scribner's Sons, 1988.

———. *Hemingway in Cuba*. Trans. Lyle Stuart. Secaucus, NJ: Lyle Stuart, 1984.

Hemingway, Ernest. *By-Line: Ernest Hemingway*. Ed. William White. New York: Touchstone, 1967.

———. "Defense of Dirty Words: A Cuban Letter." *Esquire* 2:4 (September 1934): 19, 158b, 158d.

———. "Genio After Josie: A Havana Letter." *Esquire* 2:5 (October 1934): 21–22.

———. "The Great Blue River." *Holiday* 6:1 (July 1949): 60–63, 95–97. Reprint, *True* 35 (April 1955): 21–30; Ernest Hemingway, *By-Line: Ernest Hemingway*, ed. William White (New York: Touchstone, 1967), 403–16.

"Hemingway Gets Medal: Speaks Spanish in Reply to Cuban Award for New Novel." *New York Times*, 24 September 1952, 7:1.

"Hemingway Is the Winner of Nobel Literature Prize." *New York Times*, 29 October 1954, 1:3.

"Honor Without Profit: Second-Hand Peddlers in Italy Call Hemingway's Book Best." *New York Times*, 18 August 1953, 21:3.

Manning, Robert. "Hemingway in Cuba." *Atlantic Monthly* 216:2 (August 1965): 101–8.

Poore, Charles. "Hemingway's Quality Built on a Stern Apprenticeship." *New York Times*, 29 October 1954, 1:10.

Reynolds, Michael. *Hemingway: The Final Years*. New York: W. W. Norton, 1999.

Samuelson, Arnold. *With Hemingway: A Year in Key West and in Cuba*. New York: Holt, Rinehart & Winston, 1984.

Sylvester, Bickford. "The Cuban Context of *The Old Man and the Sea*." In *Modern Critical Interpretations*: The Old Man and the Sea, ed. Harold Bloom. Philadelphia: Chelsea House, 1999. 165–84.

4

Cuban Culture: An Ethnic Background

Whereas geographical, historical, economic, and political circumstances have a profound effect upon one's life, ethnicity can be just as great a force—if not a greater force—in shaping a person's daily experiences.

The word "ethnicity" signifies the sum total of those characteristics that define a group of people by virtue of their racial and national origins, as well as the linguistic, religious, and other cultural practices that derive from those origins. During the latter part of the twentieth century, Ethnic Studies programs began and developed at colleges and universities all over the United States in an effort to understand and celebrate ethnic diversity and to promote tolerance for it. Ethnic Studies will become even more significant in the twenty-first century. As people of different ethnicities become more and more accessible to one another through travel, the Internet, and a global economy, understanding another person's ethnic background is key to successful existence on an ever-shrinking planet. *The Old Man and the Sea* provides fertile territory for the study of ethnicity and its effects upon a person's daily life because Santiago cannot be fully understood apart from his language, his religion, and those elements of his life that reflect the racial influences and national origins of the country in which he lives.

NATIONAL AND RACIAL IDENTITY

As is the case with many countries in the Western Hemisphere with a history of colonial rule, the population of Cuba descends from three distinct racial groups. Cuba was originally inhabited by the indigenous Ciboney tribe. Caucasians were introduced to the island with Christopher Columbus, who sailed from Spain in 1492. When he arrived on the island, he named it Juana after the daughter of Ferdinand and Isabella, his king and queen, who had funded the expedition across the Atlantic. The island was eventually called Cuba, a derivative of Cubanascnan, its aboriginal name. Spain then began the colonization of Cuba, establishing it as a base for further Spanish expeditions to North America.

By the middle of the sixteenth century, the native people had become all but extinct because of brutal treatment by the Caucasian colonizers, who then looked to the African slave trade to obtain the labor needed to operate plantations. Throughout the sixteenth century and during the seventeenth and eighteenth centuries, Cuba remained under the control of Spain, and the population of the island increased dramatically even as the Spanish regime became extremely repressive. By the nineteenth century, Cuba was divided into three factions. The smallest group was that of Peninsulares—white, Spanish-born merchants and plantation owners who believed that Cubans were incapable of ruling themselves. A somewhat larger group, the Criollos (Creoles), was composed of descendants of Spanish ancestors who had intermarried with either the indigenous people or the Africans brought to Cuba. The slaves of African descent comprised the third and largest group, and Afro-Cubans continue today to be the largest racial group in Cuba.

The slaves provided most of the manual labor in Cuba on plantations and mines, but they lacked legal rights and protection and lived in deplorable conditions. Because of the continuous importation of Africans, their group grew at a greater rate than the other two, and the possibility of a slave revolt posed a continual threat. Slave owners in the southern United States, in such close physical proximity to Cuba, wanted slavery to continue in that island nation for fear that any revolt or liberation of slaves would destabilize their own chattel system. In the words of Henry Clay, the secretary of state in President John Quincy Adams's administration: "This country [the United States] prefers that Cuba and Porto Rico remain dependent on Spain. This Government desires no political change of that condition" (quoted in Foner 155–56). U.S. interests were served by the Spanish rule of Cuba, which assured the preservation of slavery, but in 1844, Cuban slaves finally revolted, and they were brutally put down. Although still under Spanish rule, Cuba abolished slavery in 1886, and a decade later, the equal status of blacks and whites was proclaimed.

Santiago's remembered arm wrestling competitor, identified only as the "negro from Cienfuegos" (69) would have been drawn from that group of Cubans who were descendants of African slaves. Santiago's race is never explicitly mentioned, but it may be inferred by his very identification of this man as a Negro. In linguistic terms, Santiago "marks" his competitor by adding a racial marker to the reference to him, suggesting that the racial background of the "negro from Cienfuegos" is outside Santiago's personal racial identity. In other words, it is unlikely that Santiago would have specified the race of this man had Santiago been of the same race. That Santiago competed as he did with a man he revered as a champion of great strength suggests that in the world of this novella, poor Afro-Cubans and Cubans of Spanish descent related to each other on an equal plane.

LANGUAGE

Cuba's many years under the rule of Spain established Spanish as the country's official language. But the language as it is spoken in Cuba, and in the rest of the Western Hemisphere, came to differ in accent and vocabulary from the language that was imported from Spain. Just as the American speaker of English will recognize differences in his or her language when it is spoken by a person from England, so too will a person who is fluent in Spanish identify differences in the Spanish spoken by a person from Spain and that spoken by one from Central or South America.

In *The Old Man and the Sea*, Hemingway inserts the reader into a Spanish-speaking country and into the mind of his Spanish-speaking protagonists by having them use Spanish words and phrases. Phrases such as *qué va*, meaning "go on" or "never mind," appear throughout the novella. When Santiago produces a newspaper that has baseball scores, he tells Manolin that it came from the *bodega* (17) without translating the word into its English equivalent, a small store. Santiago is often identified merely as *viejo*; the word is an adjective that literally means "old," but in this context, *viejo* also implies both the adjective "old" and noun "man." We have already seen a parallel construction in Santiago's reference to the "negro from Cienfuegos," where the adjective "Negro" stands for the Spanish article-noun-adjective combination, *el hombre negro*. Hemingway's use of the word *viejo* connotes no disrespect in Spanish, applied as it sometimes is to men who are not actually old and here signifying a term of affection and familiarity.

Hemingway's use of Spanish also reflects Spanish-language phenomena particular to Cubans. On the very first page of the novella, we are told that Santiago is *salao* (9), a regional pronunciation of *salado*, which literally means "salty"; but as a slang term with the "d" dropped, the word signifies "bad luck." *Salao* is used particularly by Cubans to identify someone who is very unlucky.

As travel and communication between the United States and Cuba increased during the mid-twentieth century, Cubans incorporated many English words into their language, particularly in the area of baseball. Cubans also learned to adapt their Spanish to American phenomena. Santiago and Manolin refer to the *Gran Ligas* when talking about the big leagues of American baseball. Manolin also says, "But I fear the Indians of Cleveland" (17) in Hemingway's attempt to reproduce a Spanish-language sentence pattern in place of the following standard English syntax: "I'm afraid of the Cleveland Indians."

In Spanish, nouns have gender—masculine or feminine—whereas in English, most nouns are neuter. For example, "book" in English is a neuter noun, but the Spanish equivalent, *libro*, is a masculine noun. There are exceptions to the genderless nature of nouns in English, specifically in the area of terms associated with the ocean. People are apt to refer to both the sea and ships with feminine pronouns, and Santiago most often refers to the sea as a feminine entity, an association typically made by fishermen and ocean lovers alike. But on pages 29 and 30 of the novella, the narrator elaborates upon the association of the sea with both the Spanish feminine and masculine articles. *La mar*, we are told, is what the sea is called by people who love her, even if they are angered by her. *El mar*, the narrator continues, is what the younger fishermen who rely more on advanced technology such as buoys and motorboats call the sea. These men regard the sea as a masculine competitor, their adversary. Santiago, from the old tradition, however, "always thought of her as feminine and as something that gave or withheld great favours, and if she did wild or wicked things it was because she could not help them. The moon affects her as it does a woman, he thought" (30).

This reflection on the use of a definite article and what it demonstrates about the fisherman's view of the sea goes beyond elucidation of vocabulary or grammar and implies a sociosexual analysis of male-female relations. Santiago's perspective on the sea reveals his perspective on the female, a presence that, although marginalized, is represented by opposing images in *The Old Man and the Sea* and in Hispanic culture generally. Santiago's *la mar*— the fickle, wild, irrational sea—constitutes one notion of the feminine. The Virgen del Cobre (first mentioned on p. 16 of the novella in English as the "Virgin of Cobre"), associated with the religious devotion of Santiago's dead wife, constitutes another image of the feminine that is constant, faithful, and eternally pure. This icon and other religious elements embedded in the novella reflect a typically Cuban practice of Roman Catholicism.

RELIGION

In addition to the Spanish language, the Spanish colonizers brought to Cuba the Roman Catholic religion. Hemingway himself, in 1934, converted to Roman Catholicism, the religion of most Cubans until after 1959, when Castro took power and officially declared Cuba an atheist state. Hemingway, writing *The Old Man and the Sea* in the early 1950s, naturally casts Santiago as a Catholic.

Catholics believe that Jesus is God incarnate—that is, a person whose father is divine and whose mother, Mary, is human. Like persons of other Christian denominations, Catholics profess the belief in Jesus Christ as the Savior. Catholics, however, especially venerate Mary, believing that although the human person Mary physically gave birth to Jesus, she remained a virgin all her life because Jesus's paternity was divine, not human.

Roman Catholicism was the only version of Christianity until the sixteenth century when the English king Henry VIII broke with the Roman Church and formed the Church of England. The Protestant Reformation later that century increased Christians' defection from Catholicism throughout western Europe. Some of these Christians sought to reform the Catholic Church's emphases upon the saints and the Virgin Mary in prayers and devotions, emphases seen as departures from the essence of Christianity—Christ. But people in countries where Roman Catholicism continues to be practiced will demonstrate an affection for and a belief in the efficacy of the saints and Mary in their daily lives.

Catholics also believe that a person enjoys a special relationship with the saint after whom he or she is named. That person may emulate the saint's special characteristics and pray to that saint for assistance and favors, and the saint may function as a special intercessor or role model for the person who bears the saint's name. Thus, in *The Old Man and the Sea*, the name of the main character, the prayers he says, and the presence of religious pictures on the walls of his hut all signify not just Christian values, but Roman Catholic values, specifically those associated with a Cuban culture that has been influenced by both Spain and Africa.

We know the main character in *The Old Man and the Sea* by only his first name, Santiago, which alludes to a major Cuban city, itself named after a Spanish fisherman and saint. Known to some as the capital of the Caribbean, the city of Santiago is located in a natural harbor in the southeastern part of the island. Santiago functioned as Cuba's first capital during colonial times because of its highly desirable geographical location and its accessibility to the Dominican Republic, Haiti, and Puerto Rico. In pre-Castro Cuba, this city was the site of an annual festival on 25 July in honor of Santiago, the saint after whom the city was named.

Saint Santiago—also known as Saint James the Great, Saint James the Apostle, and Santiago de Compostela—was the brother of Saint John the Apostle and a fisherman who became a missionary to Spain during the early part of the first century of Christianity. He was a martyr for his faith, beheaded in A.D. 44, and his remains were buried in Compostela, Spain. Thus Santiago, the character in Hemingway's novella, can be linked with this other Santiago, a courageous—and saintly—fisherman.

Not only do Catholics invoke the help of their patron saints; they pray to Mary and, of course, to Jesus. When Santiago is reeling in his marlin, he invokes Mary's help by reciting the entire Hail Mary prayer (65), and he later promises to say another one hundred Hail Marys. This ancient prayer, specific to the Catholic Church, is based partially upon biblical text. The angel Gabriel, greeting Mary when he appeared to the young, unmarried woman and asked her to bear Jesus, the Messiah, in her womb, said, "Hail Mary, full of grace! the Lord is with Thee." Then, when the pregnant Mary went to visit her cousin Elizabeth, that woman greeted Mary with the words, "Blessed art thou among women and blessed is the fruit of thy womb." The balance of this brief prayer, "Holy Mary, Mother of God, pray for us sinners now and at the hour of our death. Amen," invokes the intercession of Mary for the person who prays. This prayer is the basis of the Rosary, a series of five groups of ten Hail Marys recited with the aid of beads that the person praying holds in his or her hands to count out the prayers. Santiago also promises to recite one hundred Our Fathers if he successfully brings the marlin to shore (87). That prayer, universal to all Christians, can also be found in the Bible as Jesus' own response to the question of how one should pray.

Another reference to Mary takes the form of the picture of the Virgen del Cobre in Santiago's hut. We are told that Santiago has taken down the picture of his dead wife, perhaps a too poignant reminder of his solitude; but he has left on his walls two religious pictures that she had hung there, implying that her interest in religion was greater than his, a phenomenon consistent with Latin American cultures where women practice their religion with greater fidelity than do men. One of the pictures that Santiago's wife hung is that of the Virgen del Cobre.

Pictures of Mary abound and are hung in Catholic homes around the world, as are pictures of Jesus. Catholics of different ethnic and national backgrounds depict Mary with the elements and values significant to their own cultures, as is the case with the Virgen del Cobre. This picture in Santiago's hut implies to those familiar with Cuban culture that he seeks the protection of Mary as she is portrayed in the Virgen del Cobre icon, and he promises to make a pilgrimage to her shrine if he succeeds in reeling in the big fish. Her likeness in statue form was discovered at sea in the seventeenth century by three boys—a comforting thought for a fisherman whose luck seems to have run out. Hemingway demonstrated his indebtedness to Cubans and their culture, which had nurtured his writing of *The Old Man and the Sea*, by dedicating his 1954 Nobel Prize for literature to the Cuban people and by placing the Nobel medal at the feet of the statue of the Virgen del Cobre in the village of El Cobre in the Oriente Province.

Catholics' devotion to the Virgen del Cobre is one of the ways in which we can see the commingling of African and Spanish influences in Cuban culture. According to David H. Brown, a contributor to *Cuban Festivals: An Illustrated Anthology*, the Virgen del Cobre had, by the beginning of the twentieth century, become associated with Ochún, the copper-skinned goddess of fertility, reproduction, love, and sweetness (92). Ochún is an *oricha*, a spirit in the Santería religion practiced by Afro-Cubans of Yoruba descent. Hundreds of thousands of people from the Yoruba tribe were brought to Cuba during the period of slavery to work on the sugar plantations, and the Yoruba expressed their devotion to the spirits of their native religion through the images available in the officially Catholic country—images of the saints, the Virgin Mary, and Jesus, whose picture in a specific form Santiago has hanging on his wall.

The other picture displayed in Santiago's hut is of the Sacred Heart of Jesus. Catholics worship Jesus as both the Son of God and the Son of Man whose suffering on the cross redeemed humanity from its sins. To sustain a visual reminder of these sufferings, Catholics have depicted the man Jesus with his heart surrounded by a crown of thorns and exposed over the clothing on his chest. This portrayal originated with Marguerite-Marie Alacoque, a seventeenth-century nun of the Visitation order in France, who claimed that Jesus asked her in a vision to propagate devotion to him depicted with his heart displayed above the garments on his chest. Special devotions to the Sacred Heart of Jesus were to be undertaken on the first Friday of every month, and any home displaying Jesus so depicted was to be blessed.

Both Santiago's relationship with the sea and his practice of Roman Catholicism reveal something about his attitude toward women. To Santiago, women are fickle and unpredictable, like the sea, or they are spiritual intercessors, like the Virgen del Cobre. In all cases, they inhabit a sphere very different from that of men, who struggle in the real world of work and rules.

Santiago unquestioningly accepts the burden of daily, difficult, solitary work as part of his perception of manhood, and when Manolin says, "It is what a man must do" (26), he articulates the machismo so prevalent in Spain and Latin America. Both men and women in traditional Spanish cultures have cultivated the notion of machismo—the idea that real men are macho, strong, and solitary beings who can endure pain without flinching. Men, so the macho ethos would have one believe, can have true friendships only with other men, particularly as they engage in activities such as work or sport or combat. Women are not capable, so macho men think, of possessing what they believe to be the essentially male characteristics of strength, endurance, and solitude; nor are women welcome in the world of sports and work that men create.

FOOD

Food is another way in which people express their ethnicity. Throughout the five days in Santiago's life depicted in *The Old Man and the Sea*, he consumes very little apart from the raw fish he eats at sea. The only actual meal described is brought to Santiago by Manolin from a small nearby café, the Terrace. The boy transports the meal in a metal container divided into two compartments, similar to the device used by "dinner boys" in Havana, who delivered prepared meals in divided containers that sometimes held embers in the lower compartment to keep the meal warm (Canova 350). Santiago's meal is composed of, as the boy tells the old man, "Black beans and rice, fried bananas, and some stew" (19). Santiago drinks a bottled Hatuey beer. In the morning, before he leaves to fish, he drinks coffee, just as he does on the morning after his return to shore. Thus Hemingway identifies typically Cuban food and beverages for Santiago to consume.

Santiago's carbohydrates constitute the staples of the Cuban diet. *Frijoles negros, arroz, y plátanos fritos* (as black beans, rice, and fried bananas are called in Spanish) are as common to Cubans as potatoes are to the Irish or spaghetti to Italians. Santiago specifically mentions yellow rice, which obtains its characteristic color from the addition of the exotic spice saffron. The combination of black beans and white rice is sometimes called *congre* or *Moros y Cristianos* (Moors and Christians) to represent the two major racial groups in Cuba—those with dark skin and those with light skin, the Afro-Cubans and the Caucasians of Spanish descent, respectively. Whereas rice and black beans are essentially carbohydrates, they also supply some protein, although not as valuable a form of protein as can be found in beef. The kind of stew that

Santiago eats is not mentioned, but most likely it is a stew made with some beef as one ingredient, or perhaps it is a stew of seafood or shrimp.

Another carbohydrate in Santiago's diet is the plantain. The banana that Santiago eats is a tropical, edible fruit eaten cooked in Caribbean countries. The banana usually eaten uncooked in the United States is a sweeter variety of the plantain. This fruit was brought to the Caribbean by the Portuguese, and the vast majority of the world's production of plantains comes from central and western Africa.

Hatuey is a Cuban brand of beer, and coffee is most often consumed in the morning as *café con leche*, or coffee mixed with a large amount of hot milk and sweetened with sugar. The Caribbean diet in general does not contain significant quantities of diary products even though coffee is typically taken with milk.

REPRESENTING THE CULTURE OF THE "OTHER"

We all see the world through the lens of our own cultural vision, and people tend to assume that their own culture functions as a norm from which all others deviate. In the United States, the majority of citizens are Caucasian, speak English, go to Christian churches. When we think of American food, we think of hot dogs, hamburgers, and apple pie. When we think of how we get things done in America, we think of our tremendous reliance on technology and the speed that technology permits and that Americans crave. Both the tendency to think of other races, languages, religions, foods, and methods of doing things as just that—*other*—and the portrayal of the "other" by a person in the dominant culture sometimes demean that which is different by making it quaint, odd, laughable, inferior, or outright wrong.

Hemingway considered Cuba his home for almost thirty years and thought of himself as thoroughly acculturated to Cuban life. He spoke Spanish, had earlier become a Roman Catholic, ate Cuban food, and fraternized with local fishermen and admired their work habits. He wrote about life in Cuba with enormous affection and enthusiasm, but as the documents in the previous chapter demonstrate, Hemingway's experience of Cuba on many levels was more like that of the tourists in *The Old Man and the Sea* than it was like Santiago's. As an affluent American, Hemingway experienced Cuba as his playground. Indeed, before Hemingway wrote this Pulitzer Prize–winning novella about a poor Cuban fisherman, all of his writing about Cuba had been for U.S. periodicals or for *American Big Game Fishing*, publications the audience of which was wealthy Americans and the purpose of which was to describe the pleasures Cuba could offer to rich tourists. How did Hemingway's situation as a non-Cuban affect his portrayal of issues surrounding Cuban ethnicity in *The Old Man and the Sea*? Or, to frame this question in terms of literary theories developed during the last quarter of the twentieth century, how did Hemingway portray the "other"?

Although the prevailing influences upon Cuban ethnicity are African and Spanish, those influences are not entirely separate in Cuban experience. The following documents present Cuban ethnicity as it has been manifested in racial origins, national heritage, language, religion, and food. The documents demonstrate varying ways of representing and understanding the same phenomena. The reader can decide whether *The Old Man and the Sea* presents Cuban culture with the sympathy and understanding of an insider or with the condescension and distance of the outsider looking down upon a culture not his own.

RACE RELATIONS: AFRO-CUBANS AND
THOSE OF SPANISH DESCENT

Santiago's brief reference to the Negro from Cienfuegos implies that Hemingway's old fisherman regarded Afro-Cubans as equals. The documents below present different perspectives on how a Cuban's race might have influenced his or her place in Cuban society. Ludwig Bemelmans's report on the position of Afro-Cubans is based on casual conversation and observation. Writing for a travel magazine, Bemelmans portrays Cuba as a pleasant place to visit, where races coexist harmoniously. Alejandro de la Fuente uses a very different methodology for a very different audience. Writing for scholars, de la Fuente derives his judgments about racism in Cuba from the careful compilation of statistics. The charts in his excerpt allow the reader to ascertain that while Afro-Cubans may have experienced equality with whites of the same—lower—social class, Cubans of African descent, such as the Negro from Cienfuegos, would not have had the opportunities for upward mobility possible for their white counterparts of Spanish descent.

FROM LUDWIG BEMELMANS, "THE BEST WAY TO SEE CUBA"

(*Holiday* 20 [1957])

"Negroes," said a Cuban to me. "They tolerate us because we tolerate them. They have favorite moving-picture theaters and restaurants and we do not go there, although they can go into any movie they choose. There are few people here who are pure white; there is some Indian or Negro blood in a surprising number of families.

"In churches nobody thinks of segregation, nor in schools. In the best restaurants any Negro is welcome. If you see one, however, in a place like Floridita, he is probably a diplomat from Haiti, a politician meeting someone, or a Negro tourist from New York who wants to find out if it's true that Negroes here are equals.

"The local Negroes and mulatoes, knowing they are treated with absolute equality and that they can go anywhere, try the elite places once or twice and then go where they are more at home."

All this I found to be true. The Negro here, a few hours away from our

Southern states, is a respected citizen and you see him as an entirely different person, unlike those you see in the South, or even in New York. The fact that he is as good as anyone allows him to be himself, unburdened by the weight that presses on the unwanted, the unloved, the tolerated and insecure; his best qualities come to the fore.

Every day I saw ten little girls in two rows passing by: they were of every shade of color, shepherded by a nun in white who was very dark. All the Negro people I have observed were meticulously clean. Cuba is a wonderful place for Negroes to spend a vacation, and should be compulsory for some of our legislators. (228)

FROM ALEJANDRO DE LA FUENTE, "RACE AND INEQUALITY IN CUBA, 1899–1981"

(Journal of Contemporary History 30:1 [January 1995])

That Cuba before 1959 was not a racist society in the United States style has been supported by a large number of scholars, who note that racial discrimination was legally prohibited; that unlike the United States, pre-revolutionary society opened some avenues of social ascent to 'coloured' people, and that Cuba had witnessed a long-term trend toward 'racial integration' during the republican period. (132)

• • •

[But] data do not support assertions of a process of 'racial integration'—in the sense of increasing racial equality—in pre-revolutionary Cuba. (139)

• • •

Higher education seemed to be the biggest barrier for non-white Cubans wanting to enter white-collar positions, for their proportional participation in those occupational categories is directly related to the rate at which they received academic degrees. The labour market did not exclude blacks and mulattoes from these positions, once the necessary educational level had been achieved. The proportion of blacks and mulattoes working in the liberal professions in 1943 (Table 10) was similar to the proportion of those with the requisite educational preparation (Table 9), which suggests that there were no discriminatory barriers affecting entry into these positions. What was really difficult was to obtain a university degree, indicating that discrimination did exist.

Participation of non-whites in the liberal professions had, in fact, in-

TABLE 9
Percentage Distribution by Race, and Index of Non-White Participation,
University Registration and Academic Degrees, Cuba, 1929–43

Speciality	Registration at the University, 1929			Academic Degree, 1943
	Whites	Blacks	Index	Index
Law	95.1	4.9	18	35'
Politics & Economics	97.0	3.0	11	—
Medicine	89.6	10.4	38	36
Pharmacy	88.4	11.6	42	32
Dental Surgery	84.9	15.1	55	60
Veterinary Medicine	94.4	5.6	20	—
Philosophy & Letters	91.8	8.2	30	—
Pedagogy	90.0	10.0	36	41
Physics-Mathematics	96.4	3.6	13	—
Chemistry	97.8	2.2	8	—
Natural Science	97.6	2.4	9	—
Civil Engineering	96.6	3.4	12	22
Electrical Engineering	98.4	1.6	6	—
Architecture	95.2	4.8	17	—
Sugar Engineering	95.4	4.6	17	—
Agricultural Expertise	92.7	7.3	26	—

Note: Index: non-white percentage in each category divided by the percentage of non-whites in the population. A perfect representation would be index = 100. For University attendance, index calculated with the proportion of non-whites in the population 14–30 years (27.65%); see *Memorias 1931*, 233. For 1943 figures, index calculated with adult population (15 years and over).
Law includes Civil Law, Public Law Lawyers, and Notary; Chemistry includes Chemical Science and Chemical Expert.
Source: Commission on Cuban Affairs, *Problems of the New Cuba*, 155. *Censo 1943*, 1035.

creased substantially since the early twentieth century, although by 1943 their representation was still well below their proportion in the working population (Table 10, A).(153)

By 1943, racial equality in the job market was far from achieved in Cuban society not only because, as has been said, non-whites were still underrepresented in the best paid occupations (and overrepresented in lower ones, such as personal and domestic services), but also because within each category, their income was systematically lower than that of whites.

Income differentials by race characterized the whole Cuban economic structure in 1943, from low-paid and largely black activities such as domestic service, to well-paid and largely white activities such as banking (Table 11, A). Public jobs were no exception, with blacks clearly employed in worse-paying occupations than whites. The economic sectors where blacks and mulattoes were less discriminated against were agri-

TABLE 10

Index of Non-White Participation, Liberal Professions and Economic Sectors, Cuba, 1899–1943

Occupation	1899	1907	1919	1931	1943
A. Professions	14	18	29	43	61
Lawyers	1	1	8	32	48
Book-keepers	2	8	–	–	55
Dentists	25	34	29	28	58
Nurses	54	36	64	33	21
Pharmacists	–	–	8	19	28
Civil Engineers	20	6	12	–	17
Teachers	11	24	39	79	71
Physicians	2	2	17	26	38
B. Economic Sector	105	103	107	107	103
Agriculture, Fishery, Mining	101	96	106	110	92
Trade and Transportation	29	32	47	79	68
Manufacturing	124	138	145	113	147
Professional Services	19	27	42	39	66
Personal Services	151	174	140	147	187
No Occupation	95	98	97	–	115
Government	45	67	67	76	77
Officials and Employees	11	18	37	74	76
Army, Police	48	68	88	80	78

Note: Index calculated with working population: 1899, 1907, 1919, 1943: 15 years and over. 1931: 14 years and over. For an explanation of the index see Table 9. A perfect non-white representation is Index = 100.

Source: War Department. *Report 1899,* 438–9, 462–3; *Censo 1907,* 513–15, 545–6; *Censo 1919,* 628–30, 662–3; *Memorias 1931,* 259–60; *Censo 1943,* 1042, 1056, 1112.

TABLE 11: Percentage Distribution, Occupational Categories, Professions and Economic Sector by Income and Race, Cuba, 1943

Category	Low Income Whites (1)	Low Income Blacks (2)	Ratio (2/1)	High Income Whites (3)	High Income Blacks (4)	Ratio (4/3)
A. Economic Sector (total)	80.2	88.0	1.1	1.8	0.9	0.5
Agriculture, Fishery	95.5	97.1	1.0	0.5	2.5	5.0
Mining	55.6	84.4	1.5	2.7	1.1	0.4
Construction	60.7	66.2	1.1	1.9	1.1	0.6
Manufacturing	74.8	82.9	1.1	1.7	1.1	0.6
Transportation, Communication	50.0	58.3	1.2	3.3	1.7	0.5
Banking	34.8	61.2	1.8	10.5	11.6	1.1
Domestic Service	91.2	96.0	1.0	0.8	0.4	0.5
Recreational Service	69.9	82.8	1.2	3.2	0.6	0.2
Professional Service	45.2	63.3	1.4	11.1	3.5	0.3
Government	55.5	67.0	1.2	2.3	0.8	0.3
B. Occupation						
Peasants	96.0	97.6	1.0	0.6	0.6	1.0
Owners, Managers	66.2	82.3	1.2	4.3	2.9	0.7
Clerks, Vendors	62.0	79.1	1.3	2.6	1.0	0.4
Trained Industrial Workers	69.9	78.2	1.1	1.7	1.0	0.6
Non-trained Industrial Workers	85.4	89.5	1.0	0.8	0.6	0.7
Security Services	83.4	85.0	1.0	1.5	0.8	0.5
Personal Services	86.0	91.2	1.1	1.4	1.1	0.8
Agricultural Workers	96.3	97.4	1.0	0.2	0.4	2.0
C. Professionals	35.4	52.1	1.5	8.4	2.5	0.1
Lawyers	20.2	40.2	2.0	23.0	5.7	0.2
Book-keepers	29.1	50.0	1.7	23.6	18.2	0.8
Dentists	20.2	23.2	1.1	12.0	10.2	0.8
Nurses	46.7	77.8	1.7	2.1	0.0	0.0
Pharmacists	44.3	43.8	1.0	6.1	12.5	2.0
Civil Engineers	8.2	18.8	2.3	43.2	0.0	0.0
Teachers	23.1	24.5	1.1	1.4	0.6	0.4
Physicians	10.3	15.2	1.5	27.8	15.2	0.6

Note: Low income, up to 59 *pesos* per month; high income, more than 200 *pesos* per month. *Source: Censo 1943*, 1098, 1203–5.

culture and fishery, activities with the largest concentration of workers in the lowest income bracket (about 96 per cent of the total).

Inequalities were larger in well-paid activities (banking, professional services) and occupations, especially among professionals, clerks and vendors (Table 11, B). In general terms it is possible to say that, the higher the occupational category, the greater the differential. Among the worst-paid occupations, those where more than 80 percent of the total labour force received a maximum of 59 *pesos* per months (i.e., peasants, agricultural workers, personal service employees and unskilled industrial workers), income differences by race were not significant. Race made little difference among the poorest in society. This tends to support the widespread belief that racial discrimination in pre-revolutionary Cuba was mainly a middle- and upper-class phenomenon. (156)

SPANISH LANGUAGE

Hemingway used numerous Spanish terms in his novella, which authenticate not only Santiago's speech and thought patterns, but also the Cuban setting in general. Of course, presumably being a native, all of Santiago's speech—as well as that of Manolin and the villagers—would have been in Spanish, so it is interesting to see where and when Hemingway opted to flavor his text with the Spanish language for English readers.

SPANISH WORDS IN *THE OLD MAN AND THE SEA* AND THEIR TRANSLATIONS

The first column below lists the Spanish words and phrases used in *The Old Man and the Sea*; the second column contains their English translations. Realize that *la* and *el* represent the definite article "the" depending upon the gender of the noun that is modified: *la* for feminine Spanish nouns, *el* for masculine. *Una* is the feminine and *uno* is the masculine of the indefinite article "a"; Spanish words ending in the letter "o" are masculine, those ending in "a" are feminine. The final vowel of the masculine indefinite article is dropped when it appears before a singular masculine noun, as in *un espuelo*.

Spanish	English
aguamala	literally: bad water (used as a common name for Portuguese man-of-war)
ay	Oh my! Ouch!
bodega	small grocery store
bonito	literally: pretty (used as a common name for a type of tuna)
brisa	breeze
calambre	painful muscle spasm
el campeón	the champion
cardel [*sic*]	possibly cord (*cordel*)
cobre	copper
dentuso	mako shark

dorado	literally: golden (used as a common name for dolphin)
un espuelo de hueso	a bone spur
galanos	highly decorated (used by Santiago as type of shark, most likely the shovelnose
gran ligas	big leagues (of baseball)
guano	a species of the palm found in Cuba
juegos	games
jota	the letter "j"
mar: el mar; la mar	the sea
qué va	Go on! Get out of here!
salao	very unlucky; regional pronunciation for *salado*
Tigres de Detroit	the Detroit Tigers
tiburón	shark
viejo	old; old man
virgen	virgin

CHARACTERISTICS OF THE SPANISH LANGUAGE AS PERSONS SUCH AS SANTIAGO AND MANOLIN MIGHT HAVE SPOKEN IT

In the excerpts from Enrique Canova's article in *National Geographic*, we see the intrusion of English words into Cuban Spanish. Spanish versions of English words have crept into Cuban Spanish via such American pastimes as baseball and via tourism. Even persons who had not been exposed to formal English-language instruction, such as those represented by Manolin and Santiago, would have adopted some English words or phrases into their predominantly Spanish speech, as did the children who were observed by Canova playing "run, sheep, run!" in a small town. At the end of *The Old Man and the Sea*, the waiter at the Terrace restaurant pronounces the word "shark" in a way that suggests how a Spanish-speaking Cuban would have brought that English word into his vocabulary. Notice that in the second Canova excerpt below, the pronunciation of *Tribune*, a daily U.S. newspaper, is confused with the Spanish word *tiburón*, meaning "shark," the very word used by the waiter to answer the tourists' question about how the marlin was ravaged. But Hemingway chose not to describe either Santiago or Manolin through their incorporation of English words into their speech.

FROM ENRIQUE CANOVA, "CUBA—THE ISLE OF ROMANCE"

(*National Geographic Magazine* 64 [1933])

The Cubans, lovers of sport, long ago adopted baseball, excelling in it to a marked degree. Years ago, when Christy Mathewson was at the height of his prowess, one of the big American teams was in Havana for training. While there it scheduled a game with the leading Cuban team.

The Americans came to the field, looking actually huge, and went rather lazily through their warming up. Then came the Cuban team, wiry little men who warmed up feverishly and proceeded to defeat the Americans before the visitors knew what it was all about: This happened time after time, and some of our best players have since been recruited from Cuban teams.

The sand-lot teams, to one who knows both languages, are a source of constant joy, for American baseball slang fitted to Spanish makes a striking jargon.

"Ess-try too!" calls the umpire, immediately to be assailed by a chorus of "Cómo ess-try too? Ni ess-try too! Eso fué una bola!"—"What do you mean, 'Strike two?' That was a ball!"

Such expressions as "fou bol" (foul ball), "homron" (home run), "ple bol" (play ball), "segundo ce-nen" (second inning), and so on, are freely used and scattered through their own slang. . . .

In smaller towns I have been amused while sitting in the parks and watching children at play.

"Ronchiflón! Ronchiflón!" screeches an excited urchin from behind my bench.

"What in the name of Máximo Gómez is *ronchiflón?*" I asked, and my idle thoughts concentrated on the game. It looked familiar, and after a while I began to see marked similarity to our own game of "run, sheep, run."

"Ronchiflón!" came the cry again. And there it was, "Run, sheep, run," with a Spanish twist to the pronunciation. (355–56)

• • •

If you are studying a menu and see the word "cotel," that is not a special Cuban drink—it is "cocktail." Best of all, I think, is the good old "Cuban" dish of "aristú." Say this rapidly, and you will find it evolves into plain, everyday "Irish stew"—which is what it is!

Sometimes Cubans' attempts to use English words result in humorous twists. I was talking to a vender near the market early one morning. Spotting the camera in my hand, he remarked:

"Do you want to take my picture? Many of the big American papers have taken it. In fact, just a year ago one of the biggest papers in the United States sent a man down here and he took my picture. He sent me a copy of it, too," he added suggestively.

"What paper was it, do you remember?" I asked.

"Sure, it was *El Tiburón*," came the startling reply, for a *tiburón* is a shark!

I did some quick thinking, trying to associate *El Tiburón* with the name of a big American paper, then asked: "You mean the *Tribune?*"

"That's it!" he cried, delightedly, "*El Tiburón*"—and I left hurriedly, for I didn't want to hurt him by laughing. (380)

RELIGION

THE VIRGEN DEL COBRE: THE LEGEND OF HER DISCOVERY

In addition to providing an insight into Catholicism as it was practiced in Cuba during the writing of *The Old Man and the Sea*, the legend surrounding the discovery of the Virgen del Cobre statue sheds light upon race relations among poor Cubans. Its discovery by three boys, two Indians and a slave, also suggests why the statue has remained an important icon, even in Castro's officially atheist state. The coppery hues of the statue appealed to those of African descent who might see in the Virgen a reflection of their Yoruba spirit, while those of Spanish and Catholic backgrounds venerate the statue as a representative of Mary, the mother of Jesus. As the legend below indicates, the fact that the statue was found undamaged at sea after a raging storm signifies to believers its association with miraculous qualities.

FROM "CUBA: OUR LADY OF CHARITY OF EL COBRE"

(University of Dayton Marian Library, www.udayton.edu/mary/ resources/engthree.html#cub, accessed 28 February 2000)

Some time around the year 1600, two native Indians, Rodrigo and Juan de Hoyos, together with a ten year old slave boy, Juan Moreno, went out looking for the salt needed to preserve the meat of the Barajagua slaughter house, which supplied the workers and inhabitants of "Santiago del Prado," now known as "El Cobre." That day they were just able to reach Cayo Francés, halfway across the Bay of Nipe, where they encamped to escape the fury of a storm which would have torn their frail canoe to pieces.

Calm was restored with daybreak, and they took to the transparent sea. In the distance, they saw a white bundle floating on the waves and approaching them slowly. At first they took it for a sea bird. As it came closer, it seemed to be a girl and at last they were able to determine that it was a statue of the Virgin Mary holding the child on her right arm and with a gold cross in her left hand. The statue was fastened to a board with the inscription, "I am the Virgin of Charity."

The Virgen de la Caridad del Cobre. From Mario
Vizcaíno, *Colección: Cultura Cubana, La Virgen
de la Caridad Patrona de Cuba* (Miami: SEPI,
1981), 27. Reproduced by permission of the
Southeast Pastoral Institute and Book Service
(SEPI).

According to the sworn testimony of witnesses, despite the recent
storm and the motion of the waves, neither the figure of the Virgin, nor
her clothing, were wet.

The head of the statue is of baked clay covered with a polished coat
of fine white powder, possibly rice paste, and the recent thorough ren-
ovation of the image revealed the fine features which countless paint
coatings had deformed. A well shaped nose and a well-proportioned face
with large, loving eyes convey a gentleness that invites trust and prayer.
The Virgin is about 16 inches high and her feet rest on a brilliant moon
whose ends surround on both side the silver cloud where three cherubs
spread their golden wings. The Child, at the left side of the statue, raises
a hand as if blessing, and in his other hand he holds a gold globe. The
entire figure is covered by a heavy cloak which gives it the typical trian-
gular shape.

The image's original clothing was white, but the faithful have given her gold and silver colored robes. Because Our Lady of Charity is a symbol of Cuban nationality, popular statues give her a white robe, a blue cloak and have the Child dressed in red: the colors of the Cuban flag. Nowadays the Virgin's dress, a copy of a very early one, is of heavy lamé with gold threads, and has the national Cuban shield embroidered on the skirt.

The simple folk have gotten used to the image of their "Cachita" with the small boat at her feet and in it the "Three Juans" who found her floating on the water. This detail is omitted in the oldest reproductions which copied the original statue.

At the request of the veterans of the War of Independence, Our Lady of Charity was declared the patroness of Cuba by Benedict XV in 1916 and solemnly crowned in the Eucharistic Congress held in Santiago de Cuba in 1936. Pope Paul VI raised her sanctuary to the category of Basilica in 1977.

CUBAN FOOD

The excerpts below from a *National Geographic* article describe the abundant repast typical of the Cuban midday meal consumed by the affluent. Refreshing drinks made from the island's natively produced fruit quench the thirst generated by a tropical climate. The scope of this midday meal makes all the more clear Santiago's poverty; he is not privileged to enjoy such a "heavy" meal. From these excerpts, the reader derives an idea of the character of Cuban food. Of all the items mentioned, the only ones Hemingway portrays Santiago eating—in addition to the fish he catches and eats raw at sea— are yellow rice, coffee, and stew. Following this excerpt are recipes for two typically Cuban foods—plantains and black beans.

FROM ENRIQUE CANOVA, "CUBA—THE ISLE OF ROMANCE"

(*National Geographic* 64 [1933])

Luncheon a Heavy Meal

The Cuban breakfast, as a rule, consists merely of coffee, toast, and perhaps fruit, marmalade, or cheese. A heavy lunch is eaten about 11 o'clock and dinner is served in the cool of the evening.

When I say a "heavy" lunch, I mean just that. For instance, I stepped into a restaurant that has been established in one location for 53 years and ordered a table d'hôte luncheon. Knowing that Cuban soup is usually a meal in itself, I chose consommé as a starter. In a few moments the waiter placed before me a huge, vaselike container with about a pint of consommé, from which I took a few spoonfuls.

"What's the matter, sir? Isn't it all right?" asked the waiter with a worried air.

"Delicious," I assured him, "but too much."

He then brought the entrée, scrambled eggs with green peas. But instead of just a taste, there must have been not less than three eggs and a man-size portion of peas, plus a huge helping of white rice which was a meal in itself.

Again I nibbled at the dish, for I was anxious to save a little room for the main course of yellow rice with pork, which is colored with saffron, seasoned with tomato, onion, green peppers, and a dash of garlic, and is really delicious.

Shaking his head sadly, as if fearing he dealt with an invalid, the waiter carried out the scarcely touched entrée and brought in a huge dinner plate piled to the edges with rice and pork and standing about three inches deep at the center.

I looked at it in some dismay, for here was enough for two or three people. However, taking a quick drink of *vino tinto* to prepare myself, I set to and did nobly by it, much to the delight of the waiter, who hovered anxiously about.

Dessert was then brought on—a half of a fresh pineapple!

Then coffee, and of course, during the meal I had consumed two huge French rolls. And all this for 75 cents. (354–55)

• • •

For the thirsty there is the "pineapple refreshment," made of freshly crushed pineapple, sugar, and water. Some order it *colada*, which means strained; others like food and drink together, and order it *sin colar* (without straining), with the pieces of crushed pineapple in the glass, a real treat.

Another pleasant drink, and one which is even more distinctive, is called *refresco de mamonsillo*. It is made the same way, but from a strange, acid little fruit with a hard shell and a huge seed. This beverage is always served strained.

Should you happen to observe strange white loaves of something stuck across the top of a glass of milk, it is only a *panal*. This is made from egg white and sugar and may be eaten separately, but is generally immersed in the milk and allowed to dissolve.

Speaking of refreshments, it is conceivable that the old Cuban *barquillo* is the grandfather of the ice cream cone. For years the Cubans served a conical-shaped, cylindrical wafer, about five or six inches long and about as big around as your finger, sticking two of these, hornlike, into each dish of ice cream. To-day they wrap three of them in tissue and lay them by the plate of cream. Some enterprising visitor may have developed the idea of making them larger and closing one end to serve as a holder for a scoopful of cream. (365)

• • •

The Emergence of the Chicken

Some years ago the Cuban chicken—I am speaking from the diner's standpoint—was an awesome thing, both as to toughness and age. As for eggs, they were small and scarce.

Despite many pessimistic warnings that conditions were not suitable for raising high-grade poultry, a number of enthusiasts began to import varieties that had proved their worth in the United States, and by proper care and feeding achieved success.

Now, practically every farmer is raising hens and eggs for his own use and to trade for pork and other products at the nearest town.

Naturally, the use of chickens as a food has expanded, although Cuba has always been famous for its *arroz con pollo*, a dish of chicken and rice.

The trading of a few eggs for store foods is not limited to the country as a means of barter, for the same method of buying from day to day, or rather from meal to meal, has long held true in the cities. A housewife will buy in the most minute quantities—two cents' worth of rice or beans, a penny's worth of salt, or five cents' worth of stew beef. Many of the stores still give *contra*, a little gift of cookies, a piece of candy, or some such trifle. (369)

RECIPES FOR TYPICALLY CUBAN FOOD

Plantains

Plantains are similar to bananas in appearance and can be found near them in most produce sections of the grocery store. Unlike bananas, plantains will not turn yellow when ripe, but rather have a brown-green, mottled appearance and feel very soft to the touch. Plantains should be peeled by first cutting about half an inch off each end and then slitting them from end to end. Cooked ripe plantains are called *platanos maduros*. Cooked green plantains are called *tostónes* or "twice-fried plantains." *Tostónes* are crisp and may be served as an appetizer or snack, but both *maduros* and *tostónes* can be served as accompaniments to a main course.

Platanos Maduros

4 very ripe plantains, peeled, cut in half lengthwise, and then divided into sections approximately 2 inches long

4 Tbs. of vegetable oil (you may substitute some butter for the oil)

salt to taste

Heat the oil in a large frying pan until it is hot (around 375 degrees). Add the ripe plantains in a single layer, cook for 3 or 4 minutes until brown, and turn with a spatula. Repeat the process on the other side, adding more oil if necessary. When the plantains

are cooked on both sides, remove them to a paper towel and sprinkle with salt. Serve immediately.

Tostónes

(4 green plantains, cut horizontally into round, half-inch pieces (as
you might cut a banana for cereal)

vegetable oil for deep frying

Heat the vegetable oil in a deep frying pan until it is very hot
(around 375 degrees). Add green plantains, making sure they are
surrounded by the oil, and cook for about 3 minutes. Remove the
plantains and place on a paper towel to drain, then press the plantains with a pancake turner or the back of a plate to flatten them.
Return the plantains to the oil for a second frying. Serve hot or at
room temperature. They will be very crisp.

Black Beans

Black beans, or *frijoles negros*, are a staple of Cuban cooking
and can be prepared as a hearty soup or served with white rice in
a dish called *moros y cristianos*, a name that reflects Cuba's two
dominant ethnic groups—the black Africans and white Spaniards.
Before cooking black beans, you should soak them in water for an
hour or two; the water should cover the beans. When all the water
is absorbed, the beans are ready for cooking.

Black Bean Soup

1 lb. soaked black beans

1 meaty hambone

1 14-oz. can of diced tomatoes

8 cups of water

3 cloves of garlic, peeled and sliced thin

1 medium onion, diced into small pieces

1 Tbs. olive oil

1 tsp. salt

½ tsp. oregano

pepper to taste

sour cream or chopped hard-boiled egg for garnish, if desired

In a large kettle, sauté the onion and garlic in olive oil until translucent. Be careful not to brown or overcook. Add the black beans, water, hambone, tomatoes, oregano, salt and pepper. Bring all ingredients to a boil, then reduce to a simmer and cook for 3 hours. Remove the hambone, pick off any remaining pieces of ham, and return the ham pieces to the soup. Use a potato masher to make the soup smoother by breaking up the beans and tomato. The soup will not have the consistency of a purée, but the beans should be very soft and somewhat broken. After serving, you may wish to garnish with a sprinkle of hard-boiled egg or a dollop of sour cream.

Black Beans

1 lb. black beans

half a medium onion, diced

1 clove garlic, peeled and sliced

2 Tbs. chopped green pepper

1 tsp. salt

1 tsp. oregano

pepper to taste

In a large saucepan, sauté the garlic, onion, and green pepper until the first two ingredients are translucent, taking care not to brown or overcook. Add the black beans and 4–5 cups of water. Bring to a boil, then reduce to a simmer. Cook for a hour or until the black beans are tender but still whole and firm. (If the beans do not seem ready, continue cooking, adding some hot water as needed to prevent burning or sticking to the pan.) At the end of cooking, most of the water will have disappeared but there may still be some liquid in the pan. Serve hot over portions of cooked white rice.

MACHISMO

Santiago's emphasis on his ability to achieve victory over the marlin by himself, without anyone's help, suggests the machismo prevalent in Latin American cultures and a legacy of Spanish heritage. Santiago's refusal to consider his pain and discomfort is also a manifestation of macho behavior. The tone of the first excerpt below, from *Hispanic*, is rather amusing, but the article tackles serious issues through a series of anecdotes that explain how the macho ethos can pervade various areas of a man's life: his perception of his physical powers, his work, his emotions, and his health.

The second set of excerpts, taken from "Power, Value, and the Ambiguous Meanings of Gender" by Marit Melhuus, presents a more scholarly approach to the issue of machismo. Melhuus provides a definition of the term and demonstrates that the assumptions about masculinity inherent in machismo also require certain contradictory assumptions about femininity. Just as Santiago describes the sea as a feminine entity that could be both generous and withholding in her bounty (30), the typical macho Hispanic man may place women in two categories: one good, one bad—a woman as either a virtuous (virginal) woman or a whore. Devotion to the Virgen del Cobre enables this dichotomizing perception of the female.

FROM GIGI ANDERS, "MACHISMO: DEAD OR ALIVE?"

(*Hispanic* 6:1 [March 1993])

"Machismo" is a Spanish word that roughly translated means he-man-ship, stud-man-ship. And while its accompanying set of behaviors can be seen in other cultures, therefore making it a universal issue, it's usually **Hispanic** men who pick up the royalties on it. It's like the Jewish mother syndrome. That is, you don't have to be a **Hispanic** man to be a machista. But it sure does help.

It all begins with power. "A lot of things that are psychological are ultimately based in biology," explains Dr. Manuel Roman, a Puerto Rican psychiatrist and psychoanalyst in the Washington, D.C., area. "Men are physically more powerful than women. And machismo is derived from the natural state of being bigger, more muscular. It has to do with dominance, autocracy, having power over others.

"A *macho* man is somebody who is expected to be sexually knowledgeable and aggressive with women, and to be fearless in his interactions with other males. The crucial point is that ideally, machismo can be a healthy, reasonable cultural coloration on the one end—running a spectrum all the way to a maladaptive emotional need in a given man. Whether all of these things are really elaborations on basic biologically determined tendencies may be at the core of it."

Dr. Raquel Cohen, a Peruvian American professor at the University of Miami, notes that in the orangutan world, dominant male behavior is built into the biology of the animal. "There's always one male in charge, and his behavior can resemble a '*macho*.' He's the biggest one; the one in the movies who bangs his chest and makes big noises. He's also in charge of the females in the group, and no male can trespass. When he gets old, a younger male takes over, but he has to fight 'el *macho*' first."

And he'd better not cry either. Machos, bestial or otherwise, are not encouraged to reveal any vulnerabilities. Amelia Castillo, the Mexican American executive director of the El Paso Senior Opportunities and Services Agency, says, "In our culture, men don't allow themselves to cry, even when it's appropriate. To them, crying is demeaning. I think the Indian would never cry. Crying is really lost energy, and this man needs his energy to be a warrior. When you drain yourself, you can never recapture it. And energy is power to continue the battle. To them, life is a war."

Life in the battlefield of the playground isn't any less hazardous for machitos-in[-]training. If they show any weakness, little boys are made to feel "like sissies" by their friends, says Adriana Kochen. The Cuban American social worker from Miami has a 9-year-old son in the third grade. "God forbid that a boy should cry in the class. When Michael gets rough and can't control himself, I always tell him, 'There's nothing better than a gentle, strong man.' I mean strong emotionally and mentally, not afraid to feel and to learn new things."

. . . [F]riction between *Hispanic* women and *macho* men both in and out of the workplace is due to a classical, ongoing contradiction in machismo [that] part of the role of the *macho*—who is also supposed to provide for his family and be loyal to and protective of them—is to prize women's virginity. Only certain women, though. Ideally, his wife was a virgin until marriage, and his daughters' virginity must be guarded at all costs. On the other hand, machistas are expected to behave seductively toward all other women (loyal, remember, but not faithful, to their wives), as long as they're not family members.

A related concept is that of respect—a peculiar kind of respect. "It's a respect that has elements of fear, awe, respect by fiat," explains Roman. "It's an entitlement, not something you earn. Like when a man tells a woman, 'You're my wife, so therefore you must agree with me at all times. Otherwise you don't respect me. You have to be loving, considerate, and never have negative thoughts about me. That's respect.' "

Must he respect her?

"That's an irrelevant concept. It goes one way here. He may unrealistically idealize her. Especially if she's a mother. But respecting in the sense of valuing what the woman has to offer intellectually, no. Because she's by definition inferior," says Roman. (2–3)

FROM MARIT MELHUUS, "POWER, VALUE, AND THE AMBIGUOUS MEANING OF GENDER"

(In *Machos, Mistresses, Madonnas: Contesting the Power of Latin American Gender Imagery*, ed. Marit Melhuus and Kristi Anne Stølen; London: Verso, 1996)

Power is usually assumed to be a male prerogative. It glosses all those attributes denoted as masculine, and represents a contested space for the articulation of masculine identity. It belongs to the penetrating realm of *machismo* and is associated with violence and aggressiveness, a particular form of self-assertion which more than anything implies being in control, being in command, having authority not only—or primarily—over women, but also over other men.

Machismo, derived from the generic term *macho*, meaning male, is used synonymously with masculinity; it implies, above all, the ability to penetrate, and is associated with being active, closed, unyielding. . . .

The stereotype of the *macho* is the violent, often drunk, unfaithful husband, or the hard-drinking, aggressive, sexually assertive young man. Concomitantly, the stereotype of the female counterpart is the self-effacing, suffering and enduring mother and the demure, withholding young lady. However, as much research indicates, these stereotypes—although they are vivid in people's minds—are no more than stereotypes. Obviously, the actual picture is much more complex. . . .

Precisely because the ideology of *machismo*—as a gloss for male dominance—is so often evoked to explain male behaviour (and, by implication, the situation of women), it is important to give a brief recapitulation of references to this term. There are several points:

1. *Machismo* underpins the continuous evaluation of men, and rests on the discrete categorization of women.

2. *Machismo* has men as its reference group: it is in the eyes of other

men that a man's manhood is confirmed, but it is through women that
it is reflected and enacted. Thus men are socially and emotionally vulnerable to other men, through the behaviour and moral evaluation of
women.

3. The very articulation of *machismo* not only points to the precarious-
ness of being a man but also underscores the ambiguity of being a
woman, showing how women's sexuality is an ambivalent source of virtue.

Finally, it is important to bear in mind that the meanings of *machismo*
are many and, in the case I am about to describe, can best be grasped
with reference to the local morality of honour and shame. This local
morality is mirrored in a specific sexual division of labour, which in turn
is reflected in specific notions of male and female virtue. . . .

Aspects of virility and women's virtue are not the only attributes of
maleness which are important for a man's respect. Values such as generosity, not being an egoist, being responsible *vis-à-vis* wife and children
in the sense of providing for them, all constitute part of the masculine
make-up and influence a man's reputation, as do his political connec-
tions, being honest, the number of godchildren he has, and his general
character. Together these aspects connote what it means locally to be a
macho in the positive sense of the word. It is precisely the notions of a
hard-working, respected and responsible man which contradict the ster-
eotypical perceptions of a *macho*. Both men and women would agree
that a man's first responsibility is to maintain his family—so much so that
a husband/father who is unable to provide for his family, or is dependent
on his wife for an income, is called a 'mantenido', literally a maintained
man, which is regarded as very unmanly. A wife who is contributing to
the household would go to great extremes to conceal her activities from
her husband, as it would be considered a shaming of his honour publicly
to display that he is not man enough to keep his family. In fact, a woman
would put up with both infidelity and maltreatment as long as she received money for the upkeep of herself and her children—*para el gasto*,
as they say.

There is also stress on a man's independence, and especially on his
being in control. The importance of these attributes is underscored by
the use of the term *lambiscon* to denote the man who is a political client,
dependent on other men, an opportunist. *Lambiscon* derives from the
verb *lamer*, to lick, or *lambisconear*, to lick or suck up to. Translated as
'greedy' and 'gluttonous' (*Collins Spanish Dictionary*), the local meaning
conveys a man without integrity, and again alludes to sexuality. *Machismo*, then, has both negative and positive connotations. It is ambiguous, multivocal, depending on the context, the situation and the man
to be described as well as the person using the term. Thus the attributes

of *machismo* which are ascribed to a young unmarried man will be different from those ascribed to a married, established man.

In order to confirm his manhood, a man needs both the virtuous woman and the . . . one who has had sexual intercourse before marriage or a child out of wedlock. This discrete categorization of women, classifying them into two kinds, is a prerequisite for this construction of masculinity. However, it is also central to the construction of female identity, but with differing connotations: whereas men need 'bad' women if they are to remain men, women need indecent women if they are to remain good. Thus female virtue is an issue which serves to underscore the differing grounds of evaluation for men and for women. Aspects of both men's and women's sexuality come into play, stressing virility for men and chastity for women. Where sexual prowess is important for men—so much so that it is considered 'falta de hombría' (lack of manhood) not to recognize illegitimate children—the converse holds true for women. Yet women do not abstain from sexual relations before marriage, even though this is the ideal. Nevertheless, the fact that sexual purity is not an issue for men, but is so for women, obviously places the woman in a more precarious position than the man. (240–44)

TOPICS FOR WRITTEN OR ORAL EXPLORATION

1. We may infer that Santiago is Caucasian of Spanish descent; lacking any evidence to the contrary, we may apply the same inference to Manolin. Examine the tables provided in the excerpt from de la Fuente's article. Using the data in the relevant time period, write a paragraph in which you speculate about Manolin's chances for upward mobility assuming that he is white; perform the same exercise, assuming that Manolin is black. Make these paragraphs as specific as possible regarding the boy's statistical probability, based upon race and gender, of obtaining an education, becoming a professional, and so forth.

2. Find a friend or classmate who is a native speaker of Spanish and have that person teach you to pronounce the Spanish words in *The Old Man and the Sea*.

3. Go to the sections of the novella where Hemingway uses a Spanish word, phrase, or syntax. Translate these portions into standard English. How does this translation affect your reading of the text? Would you have preferred that Hemingway not use Spanish in the novella? Explain your answer.

4. Hemingway does not have his characters use English words that they have absorbed into Spanish, something that might easily have been added to their dialogue when discussing baseball. What might have been the effect of including this linguistic feature in the characterization of Santiago and Manolin?

5. Attempts to render dialects in literature sometimes make speakers of nonstandard English seem comic, inferior, even villainous. Reread pages 10 through 25 of *The Old Man and the Sea*, the pages that contain the majority of the dialogue between Santiago and Manolin. Compare Hemingway's use of Spanish-language features in this portion of the novella with the uses of non-English words and phrases or dialects in the passages below:

   From Chinua Achebe's *Things Fall Apart*:

   > At last Ogbuefi Ezeugo stood up in the midst of them and bellowed four times, "*Umuofia kwenu*," and on each occasion he faced a different direction and seemed to push the air with a clenched fist. And ten thousand men answered "Yaa!" each time. (10)

   From Mark Twain's *The Adventures of Huckleberry Finn*:

   > I went to sleep, and Jim didn't call me when it was my turn. He often done that. When I waked up, just at daybreak, he

was setting there with his head betwixt his knees, moaning and mourning to himself. He was thinking about his wife and his children, away up yonder, and he was low and homesick; . . . and I do believe he cared as much for his people as white folks do for theirn. . . . He was often moaning and mourning, that way, nights, when he judged I was asleep, and saying "Po' little 'Lizabeth! Po' little Johnny! It mighty hard; I spec' I ain't ever gwyne see you no mo' no mo'!" (201)

Compare and contrast these passages, considering how the non-English or nonstandard usages contribute to and affect the setting, characterization, and tone of the literature.

6. Identify all the references to Roman Catholicism in *The Old Man and the Sea*. These references may be explicit, as, for example, to the picture of the Virgin that hangs on the wall in Santiago's shack, or implicit, as in the crosslike posture Santiago assumes when he sleeps.

   • List these references and explain how they sustain the Cuban culture of the novella.

   • Determine how these allusions affect your overall understanding of the character of Santiago and the theme of the novella. To answer this question, you should first identify the tone Hemingway employs when presenting elements of the Catholic religion.

7. Search *www.udayton.edu/mary/resources/english.html* for the description of various titles and images of the Virgin Mary. Select one title and image that represents Mary as the patroness of a particular Latin American country. Use an encyclopedia to research the basic historical, geographical, and cultural features of that country and speculate how the image of the Virgin Mary might be used in a story set in that country.

8. Determine whether your name (or a derivation of your name) is that of a saint in the Roman Catholic Church. Using the *Encyclopedia of World Religion* published by Macmillan, or any encyclopedia on religion at your disposal, look up your patron saint. In a journal entry, describe this saint's achievements. Are you similar to this person in any way? Does this saint have any traits you would like to possess? Explain.

9. Using the *Encyclopedia of World Religion*, read about some of the saints of the Roman Catholic Church. Try to rename Santiago, bearing in mind his cultural background. Would any other name suit him as well as Santiago?

10. Cast Santiago as a member of an indigenous tribe or as a member of a non-Christian religion—Judaism, Hinduism, Buddhism, or Islam, for example. Using the *Encyclopedia of World Religion*, research the

prayers and practices proper to these groups or religions. How might a believer in one such non-Christian faith appeal to a deity or higher force if super human intercession were invoked during an ordeal or in an effort to obtain a goal?

11. Think about the pictures you have hanging on the walls in your room or home and write a journal entry in which you respond to the following questions: Are these pictures of religious or historical figures, of sports personalities, of family members? Why have you chosen to hang these pictures? What do they say about your values and the culture to which you belong? If these pictures were an element in a story about you, what inferences might a reader make about your past and your values?

12. Given the natural resources on the island of Cuba, what foods besides those mentioned in *The Old Man and the Sea* might have been available to a person such as Santiago?

13. Get a Cuban cookbook from your local public library or find some Cuban recipes on-line. Cook some Cuban dishes other than those for which recipes have been given above.

14. Contrast the way in which food is presented in the excerpts above with the way in which Hemingway presents it in *The Old Man and the Sea*. Explain the ways in which the tone of these discussions of food differs in the work of fiction and in the articles written for tourists.

15. Can Santiago be completely identified with the definition of a "macho" man? Debate the issue, with one group in the class arguing that Santiago does fit the definition and the other group arguing against the idea. Consider, among other specific details from the novella, Santiago's repeated lament at sea that he wished he had brought the boy with him.

16. Finally, assess Hemingway's overall manner of portraying Cuban ethnicity. Is his depiction accurate, affectionate, condescending, something else? Use as your evidence specific information derived from the categories of race, religion, language, and food.

SUGGESTED READINGS AND WORKS CITED

Achebe, Chinua. *Things Fall Apart*. New York: Doubleday, 1959.

Barbour, Thomas. "Cuba—Country of Surprises." *Science Digest* 19 (1946): 33–36.

Bettelheim, Judith, ed. *Cuban Festivals: An Illustrated Anthology*. New York: Garland Publishing, 1993.

Brandon, George. *Santería from Africa to the New World: The Dead Sell Memories*. Bloomington: University of Indiana Press, 1993.

Brown, David H. "Annotated Glossary for Fernando Ortiz's The Afro-Cuban Festival 'Day of the Kings.' " *Cuban Festivals: An Illustrated Anthology*, ed. Judith Bettelheim. New York: Garland Publishing, 1993.

Canova, Enrique. "Cuba—The Isle of Romance." *National Geographic Magazine* 64 (1933): 344–80.

Carbajo, Antonio. *Cuban Slang: Tesauro de Cubanismos*. Miami: Language Research Press, 1968.

Connett, Eugene V., ed. *American Big Game Fishing*. New York: Derrydale Press, 1935.

Creen, Linette. *A Taste of Cuba: Recipes from the Cuban-American Community*. New York: Plume, 1994.

"Ernest Hemingway Becomes a Catholic." *Chicago Herald and Examiner*, 21 January 1934, 12.

Foner, Philip S. *A History of Cuba and Its Relations with the United States*, 1492–1845. Vol. 1. New York: International Publishers, 11.

Fuentes, Norberto. *Ernest Hemingway Rediscovered*. New York: Charles Scribner's Sons, 1988.

———. *Hemingway in Cuba*. Trans. Lyle Stuart. Secaucus, NJ: Lyle Stuart, 1984.

Hemingway, Ernest. *By-Line: Ernest Hemingway*. Ed. William White. New York: Touchstone, 1967.

———. "The Great Blue River." *Holiday* 6:1 (July 1949): 60–63, 95–97. Reprint, *True* 35 (April 1955): 21–30; Ernest Hemingway, *By-Line: Ernest Hemingway*, ed. William White (New York: Touchstone, 1967), 403–16.

———. "On the Blue Water: A Gulf Stream Letter." *Esquire* 5:4 (April 1936): 21, 184–85 (see long paragraph on p. 184 for the seed of *The Old Man and the Sea*).

———. "Out in the Stream: A Cuban Letter." *Esquire* 2:3 (August 1934): 19, 156, 158. Reprint, Ernest Hemingway, *By-Line: Ernest Hemingway*, ed. William White (New York: Touchstone, 1967), 172–78.

———. "A Visit with Hemingway: A Situation Report." *Look* 20:18 (4 September 1956): 23–31.

Manning, Robert. "Hemingway in Cuba." *Atlantic Monthly* 216:2 (August 1965): 101–8.

Pérez, Louis A., Jr. *On Becoming Cuban: Identity, Nationality, and Culture*. Chapel Hill: University of North Carolina Press, 1999.

Robinson, J. C. *Bananas and Plantains*. Wallingford, England: CAB International, 1996.

Rogal, Samuel J. *For Whom the Dinner Bell Tolls: The Role and Function of Food and Drink in the Prose of Ernest Hemingway*. San Francisco: International Scholars Publications, 1997.

Samuelson, Arnold. *With Hemingway: A Year in Key West and in Cuba*. New York: Holt, Rinehart & Winston, 1984.

"Santería." *Encyclopedia of World Religion*. Ed. Mircea Eliade. Vol. 13. New York: Macmillan, 1987.

Sylvester, Bickford. "The Cuban Context of *The Old Man and the Sea*." In *Modern Critical Interpretations: The Old Man and the Sea*, ed. Harold Bloom. Philadelphia: Chelsea House, 1999. 165–84.

Twain, Mark. *The Adventures of Huckleberry Finn*. Berkeley: University of California Press, 1985.

Urrutia Randelmann, Mary. *Memories of a Cuban Kitchen*. New York: Macmillan, 1996.

Watson, Catherine. "Heroes at Home: Ernest Hemingway in Cuba." *Star Tribune* (Minneapolis, MN), 20 February 2000.

5

Sports

Hemingway was a fan of numerous sports and an ardent sportsman in his own right. In high school, he played football, and he was an amateur boxer. After repeated trips to Spain, he became interested in the sport of bullfighting, and he fraternized with bullfighters there. In the United States and in Cuba, he followed baseball, and at Finca Vigía, he entertained figures from the world of sports. As one of the founders of the International Game Fishing Association, Hemingway engaged in efforts to elevate and regulate fishing for big game. For Santiago and the other fishermen in *The Old Man and the Sea*, fishing was a way to make a living; but for Hemingway, fishing was a sport, and the sporting ethic imbues many areas of this novella.

BULLFIGHTING TO BASEBALL

The Old Man and the Sea opens with two characters, Santiago and Manolin, engaged in a dialogue that centers largely on the subject of baseball. Indeed, this dialogue constitutes the exposition of the novella, and the characters are revealed through the value they place on baseball and its leading players. Their conversation immediately implies the bonding of men in a man's world, the world of sports. But baseball takes on special significance in the narrative structure of *The Old Man and the Sea* through a prominent series of allusions that demand the reader's understanding. As explained in Chapter 1, an allusion is normally defined as a figure of speech that makes reference to a particular historical or literary context, but the term may be broadened to include references to any body of knowledge, even in the area of popular culture—in this case, sports. A writer will employ a body of knowledge to provide some form of comparison between aspects in the narrative and those in the larger world.

Allusions to baseball help to establish this novella's setting in terms of both its place and its time. First of all, Hemingway's use of baseball in *The Old Man and the Sea* is also consistent with his insertion of this text squarely into Cuban culture. Cubans adopted baseball, an American pastime, in the process of distinguishing themselves from the culture imposed by Spain and manifested in the sport of bullfighting. This ancient contest between beast and man, still the national sport of many Spanish-speaking countries, takes place in an outdoor arena, usually on a Sunday afternoon during the spring and summer months. With a great deal of ceremony and to the sound of trumpets, the spectacle begins. The matadors (dressed in heavily embroidered silk jackets and skintight pants, and armed with only a red cape and a sword), the picadors, and the banderilleros each have a role in inciting the specially bred bulls' fury and aggressiveness. Although in some places the bullfight does not require that the matador kill the bull, as bullfighting is practiced in Spain and was practiced in Cuba, the spectacle should culminate with the bull's death.

The matador will be cheered by the crowd for his display of fearlessness, baiting the bull to pass ever closer to the matador's body. A highly regarded matador will display control over his own emotions and the bull's actions, sometimes defying the animal by turning his back on him or kneeling as the bull charges. The crowd also assesses the matador's balletlike footwork, his gracefulness, and his refusal to show fear, even though his own death or severe injury from the bull's horns is possible at any moment. Indeed, the bullfighter's demeanor represents the epitome of the Hemingway hero's characteristic "grace under pressure" (undoubtedly the reason the author became so fond of bullfighting and wrote a book about it, *Death in the Afternoon*, in 1932). When the bull has been stirred to the height of its frenzy, the matador aims for the kill.

Through the quick, precise insertion of his sword between the bull's shoulder blades, which are exposed as the animal lowers his head to charge the matador, the bull dies at the moment the matador himself is most vulnerable to death.

Louis Pérez, a scholar of Cuban culture, quotes José Martí, the great leader of the Cuban independence movement, who said that the bullfight was a "futile bloody spectacle . . . and against Cuban sentiment as being intimately linked with our colonial past." The shift from bullfighting to baseball as Cuba's national sport, then, signaled Cuba's desire for separation from Spain on all levels. "In the nineteenth century," writes Pérez, baseball "offer[ed] a measure of colonial society in transition—it was an expression of change and an agent of change" ("Between Baseball and Bullfighting" 505). Baseball appealed to Cubans because it translated the spectacle associated with the bullfight into a nonviolent arena, and the proliferation of local teams furthered the development of national allegiances during the last quarter of the nineteenth century, when Cuba made its transition away from Spanish rule.

Baseball, or *beisbol*, as it is written in Spanish to reproduce the English word with the Spanish sound, came to Cuba in 1864 with Nemesio Guilló upon his return to Havana from college in the United States (González Echevarría 90). By 1872, Cuba's first professional baseball team, the Havana Baseball Club, had been established; and by 1878, the Liga General de Baseball de la Isla de Cuba had been organized with the La Habana, Matanzas, and Almendares teams (Pérez, "Between Baseball and Bullfighting" 500). By the beginning of the twentieth century, thousands of people would attend Sunday baseball games in Havana, much to the dismay of some religious leaders who saw the sport competing with the church for popular attention. Interest in baseball spread throughout the island. Teams were sponsored by schools, social clubs, and corporations, and the sport fostered Cuba's connection with the United States (Pérez, *On Becoming Cuban* 77–83).

During the first half of the twentieth century, American baseball players—including the famous Babe Ruth in 1920—made celebrity appearances in Cuba, and many major-league players came from the United States to Cuba during the off-season to play in Cuba's professional leagues. In 1947, a pact was signed between the Cuban League and the National Association of Professional Baseball Leagues, a U.S. organization. The effect of this agreement was to turn the Cuban League into a circuit for the purpose of developing North American talent (González Echevarría 47–48). Four separate ball clubs—Almendares, Havana, Cienfuegos, and Marianao— formed the Cuban winter league, the season of which began in October and ended in February and included 144 games ("Cuban Winter Baseball League").

In addition to Americans playing on Cuban teams during the winter, Cuban players made their way to many major-league American teams. So important had baseball become to Cubans by mid-century that Castro suspended his guerrilla warfare effort against Batista during the 1957 insurrection so that his commanders might listen to radio reports from the United States about the final game of the World Series (Pérez, *On Becoming Cuban* 252–66).

But baseball as it was played in the United States in the 1950s differed significantly from the sport as it exists in the twenty-first century. The two major leagues, the American and the National, would each declare the team with the best won-lost record as the winner of that league's pennant, or flag. The two pennant winners met in October for a seven-game series to decide a World Series winner. Unlike today's complex multigame, multiteam play-off system, play-off games were held only in the event that two or more teams in either league were tied for the league lead after the competition of the regular schedule of games. Teams from opposing leagues would play each other only in practice games held during spring training before the start of the regular season. Although there were many levels of minor leagues all over the United States, Canada, and Mexico, there were only eight major-league teams in the American League and eight more in the National.

The New York Yankees were the most powerful team in baseball at midcentury, winning the World Series each year from 1949 through 1953; Santiago's confidence in the Yankees' capability reflects this fact. The Cleveland Indians were a somewhat less mighty force, winning the 1948 World Series and the 1954 American League pennant; Manolin's awareness that the Indians could pose a threat to the Yankees is thus also based upon historical fact. Several teams in the National League, including the Brooklyn Dodgers, the New York Giants, the Boston Braves, and the Philadelphia Phillies, contended for National League pennants during this same time period. There are allusions to each of these teams in *The Old Man and the Sea*.

1950 Major-League Baseball Chart

The chart below indicates all major-league baseball teams in the United States during the early 1950s and the league to which they belonged. Additional information refers to the team's explicit or implicit appearance in *The Old Man and the Sea* and the page upon which that appearance occurs in the novella. Notice that the novella contains allusions to all but four of the major-league teams playing in the 1950s. The page numbers also reveal how pervasive the allusions to Joe DiMaggio are throughout the text.

American League

New York Yankees
Joe DiMaggio's team, 1936–51 (17, 21, 22, 68, 97, 103–4)

Cleveland Indians
Seen as threat to the Yankees (17)

Detroit Tigers
Seen as potential threat to the Yankees (17)
Are playing Yanks while Santiago has the marlin hooked (67–68)

Boston Red Sox

Chicago White Sox
Santiago refers to this team when Manolin is worrying about threats to the Yankees (17)

Washington Senators
Yankees beat them on the way to the American League pennant in 1950

St. Louis Browns
George Sisler's team, 1915–30; Manolin refers to him only as Dick Sisler's father (22)

Philadelphia Athletics

National League

Brooklyn Dodgers
Santiago's favorite for the pennant (21)

New York Giants
John J. McGraw, manager, whom Santiago claims to have seen in Cuba (22)
Leo Durocher defended by Santiago as a great manager (23)
Dolf Luque's (23) team during the '33 World Series

Philadelphia Phillies
Dick Sisler's team during the 1950 National League pennant game
Santiago remembers Sisler's home run in Tropical Stadium (21)

Boston Braves
Dolf Luque's (23) team, 1914

Chicago Cubs

St. Louis Cardinals
Mike Gonzalez's (23) team

Cincinnati Reds
Santiago refers to this team when Manolin is worrying about threats to the Yankees (17)
Dolf Luque's (23) team, 1919–29

Pittsburgh Pirates

The prominent use of allusions to American baseball figures in Santiago's conversation—specifically those games mentioned on pages 17 and 21 of the novella—also establishes another aspect of setting: the specific time during which the action of the novella takes place. We already know the month in which the novella is set, September, for Santiago mentions it in conjunction with his awareness of fishing and hurricane conditions. C. Harold Hurley establishes the year as 1950. In a chapter of his edited book *Hemingway's Debt to Baseball in* The Old Man and the Sea titled "The Facts Behind the Fiction," Hurley points out this was the year that the New York Yankees played the Cleveland Indians for the pennant in the American League. Santiago expresses his absolute faith in the Yankees because of their star player, Joe DiMaggio, even though Manolin has some lingering fears about the strength of the Cleveland Indians. Both the *viejo* and the boy would have been well aware of the reports of DiMaggio's amazing comeback at the end of the summer of 1950. The two fishermen then refer to the Brooklyn Dodgers and the Philadelphia Phillies, who contended that year for the National League pennant. Although Santiago favors the Dodgers in that race, he recalls the prowess of Dick Sisler, whose most remarkable feat occurred in October 1950, something Hemingway—but not Santiago—would have known. Santiago's judgment of Sisler is derived from the fisherman's recollection of Sisler's performance when he played in Cuba, but this judgment also validates Santiago's assessment of a man's capabilities and hints at Sisler's success to come several weeks later in the 1950 baseball season. Thus Santiago and Manolin's conversation about the two pennant races in process, and about the games between the Yankees and the Indians in the American League and the Dodgers and the Phillies in the National League, fixes the dates of events in *The Old Man and the Sea*, as Hurley points out, between 12 and 16 September 1950 (77–80).

Allusions to baseball players also foster both specific and general knowledge of character in *The Old Man and the Sea*. For example, Manolin's specific age has been a matter of some speculation among critics, but in another chapter of Hurley's book titled "Just a 'Boy' or 'Already a Man'?" he settles the question to his satisfaction through an analysis of the allusions to Dick Sisler's father, George. Hurley glosses Hemingway's text and Manolin's comment as follows: "Stated more simply, Hemingway, from Manolin's perspective, means: 'the great Sisler's father [George Sisler] was never poor and he, the father, was playing in the Big Leagues when he [the son, Dick Sisler] was my age.' " Hurley determines that Dick Sisler was only ten when his father played in the big leagues; hence, Hurley concludes that Manolin is ten (97).

Whether or not Hurley is correct in his assumption that Dick Sisler is the referent of the second "he" in the sentence quoted above, baseball allusions powerfully affect the reader's general understanding of Manolin and Santiago as characters by showing us the traits these men admire in human beings: the determination to succeed and win, whatever the cost, and the refusal to let pain or bad luck affect the effort dedicated to a task. Some of the players referred to in *The Old Man and the Sea* are the legends of baseball, recognizable even to today's readers; other players would have been readily known at the time of the novella's publication; and still others constitute allusions that only someone very knowledgeable in baseball would have understood, even in 1952.

The players that Manolin and Santiago discuss and admire comprise four, sometimes overlapping categories: team managers, Cuban-born players who were managers and stars on American teams, American players who came to Cuba to play in winter leagues, and Joe DiMaggio, who, for many reasons, constitutes a category all his own. The brief biographies below will demonstrate what the characters in *The Old Man and the Sea* could (and could not) have known about each of these players at the time the novella was written.

Team Managers

Santiago and Manolin discuss who might be the greatest baseball team manager of all time. Manolin says his father thinks that John J. McGraw, who had been dead for almost twenty years at the writing of *The Old Man and the Sea*, was the greatest. Manolin asks Santiago for details about McGraw, whom Santiago claims to have seen drinking at the Terrace café and placing bets on horses. Santiago asserts that had Leo Durocher visited Cuba as many times as did McGraw, Manolin's father would favor Durocher, some of whose greatest victories in baseball would not occur until many years after the novella's publication. Then Manolin shifts the discussion to the question of the best manager—Mike Gonzalez or Dolf Luque, both Cuban-born baseball players turned managers who enjoyed great success on North American teams—asking Santiago for his judgment. But the older man dismisses the question by stating that they are equally great. The two fishermen clearly admire these managers' ability to amass numerous wins against great odds, but they must recognize that a manager's victory requires more than his own talent as a ballplayer. A good manager must be able to elicit from his players, as individuals and as a team, their best performances.

John Joseph McGraw was born on 7 April 1873 in Truxton, New York, where he pitched for the town team before joining the Baltimore Orioles in 1891. At only five feet seven inches tall and 155 pounds, McGraw quickly developed his reputation as an aggressive player with a .344 batting average. In 1901, he took on the job of managing the Orioles, and in 1902, he moved to the Giants as manager. His fiery temperament and his small stature gained him the nickname "Little Napoleon." In 1903, he led the Giants to second place in the National League and on to the pennant in 1904. Under McGraw's management, the Giants sustained their position as the most successful National League team for thirty years. McGraw is, a good eighty years after some of his greatest accomplishments, still considered by many experts to be the most successful manager ever in the history of baseball. In his thirty-year career with the Giants, the team won ten National League pennants and three world championships. This success was obtained with the help of his players' unquestioning acceptance of McGraw's authority and outbursts. He resigned as manager of the Giants in June 1932 for health reasons and died on 25 February 1934 (Stein 198).

Leo Durocher, nicknamed "The Lip" and also known for his verbal outbursts, was born in West Springfield, Massachusetts, on 27 July 1905. By the age of thirteen, Durocher was wearing custom-made suits obtained with the money he had made hustling pool. Starting his career with the major leagues in 1925, when he signed with the New York Yankees, Durocher was able to indulge himself in the pleasures of big-city life. After a stint with the Yankees, he was traded to the Reds, then he played for the Cardinals during their successes of the 1930s. Durocher made the shift to managing when he went to the Dodgers; he was named Manager of the Year in 1930, when his team finished third. In 1941, under Durocher's management, the Dodgers won their first pennant in twenty-one years. Over the course of the next five years, Durocher continued to win acclaim as a sound manager who was unafraid to bait the umps or to cross the racial divide, bringing Jackie Robinson up from the Negro League. Durocher associated with gamblers, although implications of his own gambling never led to criminal charges. He loved the glamour of Hollywood, and his reputation was tarnished when he married the actress Laraine Day before her divorce from a previous husband had become final. In baseball circles, however, even more shocking than his marriage was Durocher's move from managing the Brooklyn Dodgers to managing their arch-rival, the Brooklyn Giants.

Characters such as Santiago and Manolin discussing great managers would have had in mind Durocher's performance with the Giants during the early 1950s. His aggressive management moved the team to third place in 1950. With the addition of Willie Mays, the Giants were in the World Series in 1951, which they lost to the Yankees in the sixth game. While writing *The Old Man and the Sea*, Hemingway would not have foreseen that in 1955, Durocher would leave managing for broadcasting, then leave broadcasting to coach the Dodgers in 1960. He moved to the Cubs, again as manager, in 1966 and led the team to the 1969 World Series, where they lost to the Mets. A fiery confrontation with a Cubs player in 1970 broke the team's confidence in Durocher, and in 1971, Baseball Commissioner Bowie Kuhn presided over charges of Durocher's gambling, charges that were not substantiated. Durocher continued his career with Houston and retired from baseball in 1973. He died on 7 October 1991. *Bartlett's Familiar Quotations* attributes the following statement to Leo Durocher: "Nice guys finish last" (*Complete Baseball*).

Cuban-Born Players Who Were Managers and Stars on American Teams

In their discussion of the all-time great baseball managers, Santiago and Manolin mention Adolfo (Dolf) Luque of the Cincinnati Reds and Miguel Angel (Mike) Gonzalez of the St. Louis Cardinals, both of whom had played ball in the United States during the 1920s and 1930s. But these players had also succeeded as managers in the United States.

Dolf Luque managed teams in Latin America after he stopped playing ball in 1935. At that time, he had already enjoyed two decades of playing in the United States. Born in Havana, Cuba, in 1890, Luque, a right-handed pitcher, first played for the major leagues in 1914 during a brief stint with the Boston Braves. He then moved back to the minors for several years until 1919, when he won ten games, beginning a ten-season streak of ten-plus victories. Although 1923 may have been his best year, with twenty-seven victories for the Cincinnati Reds, which yielded him a .771 winning percentage, an undisputed high point in his career came when he pitched for the Giants during their 1933 World Series win (*Complete Baseball*). At the time of his death in 1957, Luque, then know affectionately as "Papa" (a name many applied to Hemingway at this point in his life as well), was the best-known Cuban player to have made it to the big leagues in America. The *Baseball Research Journal* calls Dolf Luque the first Hispanic star of American baseball.

Mike Gonzalez was born in 1890 in Havana and began playing ball in the United States for the New York–New Jersey Class D Long Branch team. Having made the leap to the American big leagues with the Cincinnati Reds, Gonzalez had become the starring catcher for the St. Louis Cardinals by 1917, ranking then as one of the best catchers in all of major-league baseball. In 1933, he started coaching for that team, something he did until 1946, when he returned to Havana and managed a team in Cuba. He died in 1977 (Obituary).

American Players Who Came to Cuba to Play in Winter Leagues

Dick Sisler, born on 2 November 1920, made his mark on Cuban baseball in the winter of 1945–46 by leading the Cuban League in home runs that season. He was the first player to hit the ball out of Tropical Stadium for a home run of almost 500 feet. He followed this achievement with three home runs in the game the next day. Obviously, his name and reputation were well known to Cubans in the late 1940s. Hemingway was personally acquainted with Sisler and discussed taking him deep-sea fishing, something Hemingway's characters are too humble to suggest. When Sisler returned to the United States, his lackluster career in the American big leagues had one shining moment during the last game of the 1950 season. Sisler was playing for the Philadelphia Phillies, as alluded to in *The Old Man and the Sea*. With the teams tied at 1–1 in the tenth inning against the Brooklyn Dodgers, Sisler hit a home run with two men on base, giving the Phillies their first National League pennant in thirty-five years. But Sisler did not repeat that performance in the World Series against the New York Yankees, batting 1 for 17. The Yankees shut out the Phillies to win the 1950 World Series in four games. Sisler returned to the minors as a player and manager. In 1964, he took over as manager of the Cincinnati Reds and went on to coach the Mets, Cardinals, Padres, and Yankees. He died in November 1998 (*Complete Baseball*).

George Sisler, never explicitly named in *The Old Man and the Sea*, was inducted into the Baseball Hall of Fame in 1939. The elder Sisler had a more consistent and outstanding career than did his son. Born on 24 March 1893 in Manchester, Ohio, George Sisler attended the University of Michigan and was the star collegiate baseball player of his day, although he was technically under contract with the Pittsburgh Pirates. Arguing that he was underage when he signed that contract, Sisler was released from it and went to the St. Louis Browns in 1915. As a lefty, Sisler played for the Browns for fifteen years, batting over .400 twice during that period. He retired from baseball in 1930 (Dewey and Acocella 427–28).

Joe DiMaggio

This legendary baseball figure, still widely recognized today, warrants a category all his own because of his enormous fame as a baseball player and his importance to the theme of Hemingway's novella.

Joseph Paul DiMaggio was born in Martinez, California, in 1914 to parents who had immigrated from Sicily. His father was a fisherman, and the family settled in San Francisco, where DiMaggio grew up. He was playing for the minors in the early 1930s when he began to demonstrate amazing ability during the 1933 season, obtaining at least one hit in each of sixty-one consecutive games for the San Francisco Seals. In 1936, during the era of such baseball greats as Babe Ruth and Lou Gehrig, DiMaggio went to the Yankees to play center field. During his rookie season, he batted .323, with 29 home runs and 125 runs batted in (RBIs). His stats during the following year were even better, with a .346 batting average, 46 home runs, and 167 RBIs. In 1939—the year he married Dorothy Allsford, with whom he had one child—DiMaggio was named the American League's Most Valuable Player (MVP), with a career high batting average of .381. The year of DiMaggio's great hitting streak in the majors was 1941; he had fifty-six hits in consecutive games for the Yankees. The streak ended during a game with the Cleveland Indians on 17 July. (The ability to break DiMaggio's hitting streak would have been grounds for Manolin's fear of the Cleveland Indians.) But on 18 July 1941, DiMaggio began a new, sixteen-game hitting streak, and he earned his second MVP award that year.

DiMaggio served in the armed forces during World War II, and he and his wife divorced in 1944. At the close of the war, he returned to the Yankees and won his third MVP award in 1947. But by the end of the 1940s, injuries began to plague DiMaggio, who missed the first half of the '49 season due to surgery for bone spurs in his right heel. His recovery was slow and painful, and many, including DiMaggio himself, began to wonder if he would ever play again; but after a sixty-five-game absence, Joe DiMaggio returned to the plate. In the first game, he hit a home run. During the next game, DiMaggio hit two home runs; and in his third game, he hit yet another homer. In this three-game period, DiMaggio hit four home runs, drove in nine runs, and caught thirteen fly balls—an amazing comeback and an amazing role model for Santiago.

DiMaggio had certainly earned his nicknames the "Yankee Clipper" and "Joltin' Joe." By the time DiMaggio retired in 1951, he had been the Yankees's star player during the period when they won nine World Series. Elected to the National Baseball Hall of Fame in 1955, he was named baseball's "Greatest Living Player" in 1969. DiMaggio was known for his cool demeanor, his apparently effortless technique as a center fielder, and his stoical ability to play even when injured and in great physical pain. In many ways, DiMaggio embodied the "grace under pressure" code of the Hemingway hero.

Like other baseball players who had been drawn to Hollywood glamour, DiMaggio married an actress. In 1954, he married Marilyn Monroe, a marriage that lasted only nine months. But he remained devoted to her. It was rumored that a reconciliation was in sight before she committed suicide in 1962, and it was Joe DiMaggio who arranged for Marilyn Monroe's funeral. Recent biographies by Donald Spoto of Marilyn Monroe and by Richard Ben Cramer of

DiMaggio reveal a dark side to the Yankee Clipper. He could be venal in his desire to capitalize upon his reputation, and he had become estranged from his only son, a man who died homeless before his father's death in 1999. But DiMaggio's name remains a synonym for excellence in baseball ("DiMaggio, Joe").

Santiago thinks repeatedly about DiMaggio, not merely because the player was a legend in his own time, but because, as the son of a poor fisherman and a man who had come back to baseball after physical injury and a streak of bad luck, DiMaggio offers Santiago personal inspiration. Clearly, Santiago's interest in DiMaggio goes beyond admiration for the baseball player's skill. The fisherman identifies with the ballplayer's ability to transcend his physical ailments, and Santiago hopes this identification will include his own ability to recoup former glory. When Santiago's confidence falters, he thinks of DiMaggio. When Santiago is in pain—one hand cramping, the other cut, his back aching—he recalls DiMaggio's bone spurs, believing that the baseball player has performed spectacularly notwithstanding his pain. Thus thinking about DiMaggio inspires Santiago to strengthen his resolve, to struggle in spite of pain, and to hold on to hope when reversal of bad fortune would otherwise seem impossible.

In "Santiago at the Plate: Baseball and *The Old Man and the Sea*," James Plath performs a thorough examination of the ways in which baseball frames the narrative structure of the novella. Plath points out that the protagonist's devotion to DiMaggio performs a quasi-religious function. Although Santiago possesses the trappings of a Catholic—he prays Catholic prayers, he has Catholic pictures on his wall—he admits to not being a religious man. Religion does not comfort Santiago; baseball does. Plath argues that Santiago not only admires DiMaggio, he wishes to be "worthy" of him, an interesting sentiment considering that the fisherman is not known to the ballplayer. But in some perception of a transcendent connection, Santiago wishes to perform all his activities with the discipline, precision, and care that would make DiMaggio proud of him, if he but knew him (Plath 65–83).

ARM WRESTLING

Arm wrestling also constitutes a sport that takes on importance in Santiago's recollections. He strengthens himself to continue his battle with the gigantic marlin by recalling his victorious arm wrestling match with the "negro from Cienfuegos." Santiago claims that the match lasted one day and one night, with referees spelling one another so that they could sleep. Santiago further claims that his opponent's fingernails seeped blood because of the intensity of their mutual struggle. But against the odds, Santiago bested this formidable opponent, as he convinces himself he will again conquer another opponent.

Once again, Hemingway creates an appropriate cultural ambience by using a sport that is tied to indigenous North American history. The origins of arm wrestling are attributed to Native American peoples. This sport can be practiced easily. It needs no special equipment or field, and men can engage in it informally at bars and in workplaces, displaying sheer strength and machismo. Formal, organized competitions, however, stipulate rules and weight categories. A match, known as a "pull," involves the two competitors seated at a table, arms upright in a V shape, hands gripped with the knuckles facing out. A competitor seeks to force the opponent's hand to the table; this is know as a "pin." According to the *Encyclopedia of World Sport*, a pull generally lasts less than a minute. Record-making pulls have lasted several minutes ("Arm Wrestling" 47–50).

Santiago's claim that his arm wrestling match lasted one day and one night is clearly an exaggeration of what is possible in that sport. A twenty-four-hour period is comprised of 1,440 minutes. Therefore, Santiago claims that his competition with the Negro from Cienfuegos lasted 1,439 times longer than the duration of a typical pull. This statement seems to exceed mere exaggeration and verge upon fantasy. But Santiago's memory of the arm wrestling competition, like his struggle with the marlin and that fish's great size, is consistent with a narrative that posits that a human being can perform truly superhuman acts.

FISHING

Although Santiago's combat with the great marlin and his memory of the arm wrestling competition assume epic proportions, his ritualized, deliberate actions as a fisherman are governed by the respect for established boundaries, for the rules and the fair play that one would expect from a serious game fisherman. Fishing is not a game for Santiago, but his actions and attitudes do reflect those of a sportsman.

Hemingway, an ardent sport fisherman, had written extensively about fishing for marlin in the waters off the Cuban shores. In "Marlin Off the Morro: A Cuban Letter," first published in the autumn 1933 issue of *Esquire*, Hemingway describes what was for him then a newly discovered pastime. Hemingway enjoyed the extensive marlin fishing season—spring through the end of the summer. During the midsummer months, Hemingway claims in his letter, a fisherman could daily catch a 300-pound marlin. Hemingway then documents what he knew to be the record marlin catch by a commercial fisherman to that date: 1,175 pounds of dressed fish. Hemingway marvels at the thought of this fish jumping and questions what this marlin must have weighed before he was gutted and his head and tail were cut off (Hemingway, *By-Line* 142–43).

Marlin provided sport fishermen with particular challenges and pleasures. Hemingway's passion for game fishing, and specifically fishing for marlin, prompted him to become one of the founders of the International Game Fishing Association in 1939; in 1950, he began the International Marlin Tournament in Cuba, later renamed the Hemingway Tournament, an event that occasioned his only meeting with Fidel Castro in 1960, when the Cuban leader participated in and won that competition.

The question of how to determine and calculate the weight of fish for the record was something pondered by sport fishermen who participated in fishing competitions. Thomas Aitken, the editor of a regular column titled "Big Game Fishing" in *Outdoor Life*, had queried his readers' positions on "mutilated fish"—that is, game catches that had been attacked by other fish, particularly sharks, before being brought to shore to be weighed. Aitken published Hemingway's response to this question in 1936 under the title "Hemingway on Mutilated Fish."

In this article, Hemingway discusses several factors that affect the calculation of the weight of a game catch and the criteria for awarding the fisherman a trophy in competition. Hemingway classifies game fishermen into two groups: those who reel in the fish entirely through their own skill and effort and those who employ the assistance of others—the members of a pleasure boat crew, for example. Hemingway also remarks that after the fish is hooked, it is frequently mutilated or lost entirely to sharks, often because the fisherman is too fatigued to sustain the fight. If the sharks are the agents of the fish's death, then Hemingway believes the fisherman should not get credit for the catch; but if the fish is attacked after it has been gaffed by the fisherman, then Hemingway believes the fisherman should be credited with the kill, knowing that the loss of blood and weight caused by the shark attack will affect the fish's weight calculation in the tournament and the fisherman will consequently be penalized.

Hemingway speaks with the authority and sympathy of one whose catches have frequently met the fate of sharks. Gaffing causes the fish to bleed, says Hemingway, and bleeding draws a shark attack, an occurrence made all the more difficult to fend off because of the rough seas that churn up so predictably in the late afternoon off Cuba's shores. Nonetheless, Hemingway concludes his remarks by pointing out that "nobody is going to put in [the record books] fish that are half eaten, and then dragged out of the ocean, as records" (70–72). Although articulated for the purpose of judging a game-fishing catch, this statement also renders a judgment on Santiago's achievement. No matter how much his marlin may have weighed when Santiago caught it, the mutilated carcass earns him no money. Neither does it earn him any acclaim or victory. Furthermore, his assertion that his catch weighed 1,500 pounds or more is based on nothing but an estimate that was calculated in moments of enormous fatigue and exertion. No one but Santiago saw the fish before it was mutilated. No one weighed this fish by any means that could establish its weight or size.

GAMBLING

Gambling is, perhaps, an unfortunate topic to find its way into a chapter on sport, but it is a subject inevitably associated with sporting events, even though betting on professional sports is still illegal in the United States. Gambling in nightclubs, as was discussed in Chapter 3, sustained Cuba's economy by drawing tourists from the United States. But Cubans such as Santiago engaged in forms of gambling other than those that drew tourists to nightclubs and casinos. For example, Santiago considers whether his eighty-five-day streak of bad luck in fishing could be converted into good luck by purchasing a lottery ticket with that number, and we know that the observers of his arm wrestling match waged bets for the winner. These forms of gambling—lotteries and betting on sports—have typically been available to the lower and middle classes in society.

Moreover, gambling is associated with the baseball players identified in *The Old Man and the Sea*. Santiago says he saw John J. McGraw place bets on horses, and Leo Durocher had charges of gambling brought against him, even though those charges did not result in criminal convictions. The most notorious instance of gambling in professional major-league baseball in the United States was exposed immediately after the 1919 World Series. It was discovered that several members of the Chicago White Sox (forever after known as the Chicago Black Sox) had deliberately lost in order to hedge bets for gamblers. Although Manolin mentions the White Sox as contenders for the American League pennant in 1950, no specific reference is made in *The Old Man and the Sea* to the 1919 scandal.

The gambler is one who seeks to benefit from good luck and to avoid bad luck. Profits gained from gambling are not due to an individual's expertise, talent, effort, or character. In many significant ways, the gambler approaches success from exactly the opposite path used by the careful practitioner of a craft. Santiago's patience and his expertise, gained from a life of experience as a fisherman, should bring about his success as a fisherman. Yet he acknowledges the role of pure luck in his endeavors. Luck, specifically bad luck, causes his painfully long catchless streak; Santiago talks to Manolin about lucky and unlucky boats; and the old man conceives of the giant fish as his good luck. "He is my fortune" (95), says Santiago, creating a pun on the word "fortune." The marlin will confirm Santiago's good luck, his good fortune, and the marlin will bring Santiago a fortune, much money, at the market.

The sporting ethos pervades *The Old Man and the Sea*, and the documents that follow provide the reader with a better understanding of the novella's major characters by helping us to know, as they did, the baseball figures they so admired. The novella alludes to events involving baseball personalities widely known to contemporary audiences; other baseball allusions required glossing for the audience reading *The Old Man and the Sea* at the moment of its publication. These figures represent, even for the *viejo* Santiago, the good old days of baseball. And, as we shall see, baseball fans in the late 1940s and early 1950s would have known about the not always admirable features of these baseball players' personalities. Furthermore, the sport of game fishing is very much in evidence in this novella, even though Santiago is a commercial fisherman. When we try to assess Santiago's achievement, we must do so by some standard. Documentation of the regulation of game fishing suggests a thematic interpretation of the novella by giving us a yardstick by which to measure Santiago's catch.

BASEBALL

JOHN J. MCGRAW'S STYLE AS MANAGER

In the excerpts from the article below, Joe Williams praises Mc-Graw's talents as a manager and builds a picture of a colorful character. His depiction of McGraw allows the reader to understand why he would have been among the managers Santiago and Manolin identified as the best of all time; but the reader can also see that McGraw was known for his flamboyant character and outbursts.

FROM JOE WILLIAMS, "THE PASSING OF MR. McGRAW, MAYBE
IT'S FOR THE BEST, GIANTS NO LONGER HIS GANG"

(*New York World Telegram Sports*, 4 June 1932)

After thirty years of continuous services John Joseph McGraw has resigned as manager of the Giants, leaving behind a glorious record as a player, team leader and personality.

At the age of 59 Mr. McGraw steps down because of failing health, with his Giants in last place, apparently headed for no place in particular—an ironical climax of a career marked by many successes and a stern intolerance for mediocrity.

Mr. McGraw is possessed of all the normal vanities that successful leaders develop. He is vain about his position in baseball, his records as a builder of championship teams, his distinction as the Master Mind and the Little Napoleon. . . .

The game offered no more stirring spectacle in the old days at the Polo Grounds than the short, stocky figure of Mr. McGraw moving toward the home plate umpire with a chip on his shoulder and a quip on his lips. It was, somehow, a natural part of the Giant picture. When Mr. McGraw failed to fly into the face of an umpire over a close decision that went the other way the customers became suspicious and alarmed—either something was desperately wrong with the manager or the game itself was slipping.

It is not a part of the records that Mr. McGraw ever won one of these blazing battles of the mouth, nor is it in the records that he ever quit trying. In everything his slogan was to go all the way, run everything out and battle for your rights—even when you are wrong. To the end Mr. McGraw was faithful to his truculent creed. . . .

• • •

His Real Greatness

Mr. McGraw was a product of the old school of baseball, when fist fights were common, when red liquor was sold in all the parks, when only ladies of questionable social standing attended the game. He was a black-haired, pasty-faced young Irishman to whom roughhouse tactics were merely a part of the trade. It was a fighting game in which only fighting men survived.

Mr. McGraw became distinguished for his fiery exploits which bordered on rowdyism. Somebody tagged him Muggsy. For years he was Muggsy, of the Giants, an appellation betokening warmth and affection on the part of his disciples. But as the game gradually emerged from its primitive crudeness Mr. McGraw softened and changed with it.

As a matter of fact, Mr. McGraw had two personalities; off the field he was usually soft spoken, reticent and congenial. The exceptions were when the gentleman tarried too long at the festal board and heated controveries about this and that developed—but these are exceptions common in the lives of all active festal boarders.

Mr. McGraw's record as a team leader speaks for itself. To my mind it is the least of his greatness. No man in the history of baseball has been more generous or more kindly to friends in distress. His charities to down and outs, ball players, fighters, jockeys—good fellows when they had it—have been enormous.

They say of him: "He's the toughest loser in the world and the easiest guy to touch." (7)

LEO DUROCHER'S PERSONALITY AND PLAY IN CUBAN BASEBALL AND IN THE UNITED STATES

Like the much-admired John McGraw, Leo Durocher was a highly effective manager and player also known for his verbal outbursts.

The excerpt from *Collier's* provides a glimpse of Cuban baseball in addition to its spotlight on Durocher. First, the article documents the consequences of Durocher's argument with an umpire when he played ball in Havana's Tropical Stadium. Not only was Durocher ejected from the game, he was escorted from the field by the military, something that has never yet occurred in a ballpark in the United States. In addition to Durocher, almost all of the players mentioned in *The Old Man and the Sea* are cited in this article. It is noteworthy that "Play Ball, Amigos" was published during the very period in which Hemingway was conceiving his novella.

According to Roberto González Echevarría, an author on the history of Latin baseball in the United States, that subject has been dealt with "lightly and condescendingly" (6)—a trend he hoped to correct in his book *The Pride of Havana*. Read the excerpt from *Collier's* below with an eye toward determining if its reporting of Cuban baseball might have contributed to the Stateside reader's attitude of levity and condescension. Is this an attitude toward baseball that surfaces in *The Old Man and the Sea*?

Finally, notice also that the subject of gambling is openly discussed in association with Cuban baseball in the second excerpt; the first excerpt also mentions gambling and Durocher's association with it.

FROM "PLAY BALL, AMIGOS: WHEN YUBA PLAYS BALL DOWN IN CUBA, ANYTHING GOES"

(*Collier's*, 20 January 1951)

Leo Durocher was arguing with an umpire, practically a reflex action with the Lip, even back in 1942. Eventually, the umpire wearied, as all umpires must, and decorated Leo with the Order of the Thumb. Durocher lingered for a final word, but this was a Cuban umpire and at his gesture a couple of soldiers appeared behind Leo, pointed fixed bayonets at the seat of his pants and growled a few words. The Lip went, and stood not upon the order of his going. Durocher doesn't understand Spanish but cold steel has a language which is universal.

It was a long walk, some 500 feet, to the left-field clubhouse in Havana's La Tropical Stadium. Every time Leo whirled to shout something at the umpire, the bayonets prodded him on his way. The 10,000 fans whistled shrilly at every foot of the journey, the whistle being the *habaneros'* equivalent of the boo, the jeer, the catcall and the Bronx cheer.

So far, no National League umpire has had to call out the militia to drive home a point in a debate with Durocher, but umpires in Cuba learned long ago that it pays to be prepared. The Cuban player is likely to be somewhat more impulsive and impetuous than his North American counterpart, and the Cuban fan is far more demonstrative than his brethren in the States.

In some American cities, notably Brooklyn, a fan's enthusiasm sometimes reaches a point, particularly around Independence Day, when he feels impelled to toss a lighted firecracker on the playing field. The fan feels there is something extremely amusing about the leap of an enemy coach as a two-inch salute explodes behind him in the coachers' box. But no major-league fan, not even in Ebbets Field, has yet reached the point where his exuberance caused him to set a skyrocket swooshing into the air during a game, a practice which is looked upon with favor in Havana.

The bald truth of the matter is that fans in the United States and/or Brooklyn must take a back seat to the Cubans in baseball enthusiasm. One fan threatened to kill himself if his team lost—and did! Another, clad only in a covering of Mercurochrome, ascended a tree in the heart of downtown Havana, vowing to remain there until the Lions, who had lost five in a row, ended his disgrace. A city judge approved a petition for divorce on grounds of incompatibility—the husband rooted for Almendares, the wife for Havana. . . .

So sorely beset were the Havana police and military at a Ladies' Night when those bitter rivals, Almendares and Havana, played at Gran Stadium in downtown Havana that the police department made a formal request to the league that these teams never be scheduled on a night when the female fans were to be admitted free. The league, having had a taste of dynamite, agreed never again to put such a burden upon the police. . . .

There is, as might be expected in a country in which there is a federal lottery with tickets sold on every street corner, considerable gambling on Cuban baseball games. There are those who insist that there is just as much gambling on baseball in the United States, which well may be so, but in Cuba the wagering is not undercover. . . .

The pool hustlers and the bookies are colorful characters. *El Sopo* (Soupy) was long a favorite around the Havana ball parks for his raucous voice and his winning gold-toothed smile. He was a streetcar conductor in civil life and wore his uniform while selling tickets as well as while collecting them. Another, with a wooden leg, had a fistful of bills, which he kept folded lengthwise between his knuckles. He made friends with the visiting writers and always managed to obtain the names of the pitchers in advance. This was good judgment since all big-league managers at the start of spring training used pitchers only three innings at a stretch and Peg Leg would arrange his betting odds to suit the pitching rotation.

Gambling, of course, is frowned on in American baseball but every once in so often an ambitious D.A. rounds up a bookie and throws him in the clink, learning in subsequent disclosures that the bookie has been handling thousands and hundreds of thousands of bets on ball games throughout the country.

That the enthusiasm of the Cuban for baseball stems from gambling isn't wholly true. Whether in Havana or in Chicago, a rooter with a bet on a ball game is obviously going to be more intense in his feelings, but in Havana, as in Chicago or elsewhere, the percentage of spectators with a bet riding is small. The only real difference is that in Cuba the betting is not furtive.

A ballplayer enjoys far more prestige in Havana than he does here in the cradle of baseball. Part of this is due to the national pride Cubans felt in its early pioneers who made good in the major leagues—Adolfo Luque, Miguel Gonzalez, Baldomero Acosta. These men were able to return to their native island wealthy by Cuban standards. (34)

• • •

The Cuban Winter League, current outlet for the volatile emotions of Cuba's fandom, is unique. Quite possibly it plays the fastest ball of any league in the world, outside of the majors, of course. Now that it has made peace with the commissioner's office, the American importations to the loop are limited to 10 to each club. Major-league clubs may be represented by two players, provided they have no more than 45 days' major-league experience in the past season to their credit. Since a major-leaguer with no more than 45 days' experience is something of a rarity, practically all of the Americans in the league are from the minors.

The league is composed of four clubs—Havana, Almendares, Marianao and Cienfuegos—and all games are played in the newly constructed Gran Stadium in Havana. Almendares and Marianao are suburbs of Havana, while Cienfuegos is 130 miles away. . . .

American players are well paid. For this much shorter season comprising 72 games and running from late October to mid-February, they receive precisely the same salary as they received in organized ball for the long summer season, plus $350-a-month living expenses. The set expense sum was arrived at by league officials when they discovered that some American players would establish themselves and their families in a suite at the swank Hotel Nacional for the first few days, then move to a more modest establishment, but they would continue to bill the league at the original rate. (69)

• • •

Before Gran Stadium was built five years ago, the league held forth at La Tropical, three miles from the center of town. La Tropical was even more spacious as to playing area than its successor, but seated only 20,000. Gran Stadium's lighting system is an excellent one, better than those in several of the topflight minor-league parks in the States.

At the concessions stands at Gran Stadium, or from the vendors who hawk their way noisily through the stands, a fan may purchase any of the edibles and potables we consider indispensable to baseball here in the States—peanuts, popcorn, hot dogs, ice cream and pop. He also may purchase genuine hot tamales, hamburgers or Cuban coffee, thick and sirupy, served in demitasses.

American visitors are warned to take their hot dogs and hamburgers with care, for, with true Cuban hospitality, they are likely to be served with every imaginable sauce and condiment, to say nothing of several unimagined. Catsup, relish, chili, diced onions and mustard all are served with hot dogs, as well as this improbable added starter—a spoonful of dry corn flakes! Not bad, either.

Mike Gonzalez, who coached at third base for so many years for the Cardinals, is the Connie Mack of Cuba. He manages and owns the Havana Lions and is said to average a $40,000 profit per season. That is considerably more than Mike got for directing traffic around third base for the Cardinals. The franchise is valued at $300,000 and it is easy to see why Gonzalez has no burning desire to return to the majors.

Even the prestige of Gonzalez is no guarantee of immunity when the fans think he has called one wrong. The winter before last, Miguel allowed one of his batters to hit away when the situation seemed to call for a bunt. The play backfired, as baseball gambles so often do, and an irate fan waving a red banner charged on the field and berated Gonzalez as "a traitor to Havana." . . .

The enthusiasm of the Cuban for baseball is no new thing. John McGraw visited there in 1890 as part of a barnstorming team of Americans. At that time, the Cubans, still under Spanish rule, had not progressed enough to field their own teams and the games were exhibitions between groups of strolling American players. By 1911, when McGraw came back with his Giants, just after they had lost the World Series to the Athletics, the Cubans had developed to the point where they were able to give the National League champions a great run for it.

The Havana Reds beat the Giants in the first two games and when the series with Almendares opened, the National Leaguers got a typical McGravian tongue-lashing. Among other things, they were told that if they didn't win that day, they could pack up and go home—and at their own expense. (70)

THE CUBAN PERCEPTION OF DICK SISLER

Although Dick Sisler did not become a Hall of Famer like his father, he was far better known to Cubans than was George Sisler. Like many other American baseball players, Dick Sisler honed his skills by playing in the Cuban Winter League. The article below is a U.S. account of Sisler's spectacular home run in Tropical Stadium, exactly what Santiago and Manolin would have had in mind as they spoke of him.

"SISLER'S SON HITTING STAR IN HAVANA"

(World Telegram, 29 January 1946)

By the United Press.

HAVANA, Jan. 29.—The sports idol of Cuba today was lusty-hitting Dick Sisler of the Havana baseball team, son of the great American League first baseman and a batting star in his own right.

Now holding an average of .330, young Sisler, within a month of his arrival here, shattered a home run record which had stood in Cuba for 26 years when he pelted three four-baggers in a single afternoon.

And the day before that, he established a new Havana League record for distance when he walloped one over the Tropical Stadium right field fence that carried more than 450 feet. Before the war, there was a standing prize of $1000 for such a feat, but Sisler's only reward was a gold watch.

Dick belongs to the St. Louis Cardinals and although he never has played in the big time before he is slated for close consideration this spring.

Wife Credits Sleep for Dick's Slugging

Dorothy Sisler, Dick's young wife, attributes his heavy hitting to plenty of sleep. The night before he poled his 450-foot drive, he retired at 8:30 p.m. and was in the hay at 8 sharp on the eve of his three-homer performance.

Sisler now leads the Havana League in homers and triples. In his first 91 times at bat, he rapped out 30 hits for 51 bases and scored 19 runs. He drove in 18 others. His extra base record is six homers, five triples and seven doubles.

Dick spent 37 months in the Navy before his arrival here. His brief prewar baseball career included service with Washington of the University League, a Class D outfit, Lansing, Mich., (Class C) and several Class B clubs in the South. He graduated to Sacramento, Calif., of the Pacific Coast League just before he entered the Navy.

JOE DIMAGGIO

The excerpt below documents the enormous impact Joe DiMaggio had upon baseball during the 1950 and '51 seasons, the period when *The Old Man and the Sea* was set and composed. Dan Daniel's article features the famous Yankee's own speculations about the direction his career might take. Notwithstanding his comeback during the 1950 season, DiMaggio's comments reveal that he recognized that he was aging out of his profession, a fear both Santiago and his creator experienced during the writing of *The Old Man and the Sea*. As was typical for him, Daniel refers to DiMaggio as "Giuseppe," the Italian version of the first name Joseph. The article parallels DiMaggio to Santiago in interesting ways: DiMaggio admits to living a lonely life as a baseball player, and he discusses a successor, Mickey Mantle, who, though nineteen years of age at the time, is referred to as "the boy."

FROM DAN DANIEL, " 'MAY BE MY LAST YEAR:' DIMAGGIO"

(*World Telegraph Sun*, 3 March 1951)

Phoenix, March 3—Joe DiMaggio, most spectacular ballplayer of his time, and, since 1936, worthy successor to Babe Ruth, is contemplating retirement, not only from the Yankees but from all connection with the game at the close of the 1951 season, he reported today.

"This might be my last year," said DiMaggio. He had been asked how many more campaigns lay before him with the Bombers.

"I would like to have a good year and then hang them up," Giuseppe continued. "I would not want to fade out gradually."

When queried about the possibility of a managerial career, DiMaggio disclaimed such ambitions.

"I have absolutely no idea of managing a ball club," Joe stated. "I have plenty of headaches running myself, and would not be interested in directing a group of players.

"I doubtless could go right on playing ball for some years to come. I am not, as some writers have insisted, a brittle ballplayer. I never have been. I am a good tough-boned guy.

"For 12 years I have played a lot of ball games, with all my injuries. To be exact 1620 of them. Last season I got into 139.

"They said a year ago that I would not be able to play 100 games. Now they are writing the same thing."

DiMaggio halted for a moment, then laughed. "Who knows? I might run into a bad season and not be able to buy a base hit. But that brittle stuff is out."

Joe said that he had not discussed his retirement plan with anybody connected with the club. "I don't have to talk about it with them, they feel it coming," he added.

"I put my whole heart into the game, always," DiMaggio continued. "During the season I lead a pretty lonely life. I don't mind that. I concentrate on baseball. Maybe I take it too seriously."

"Is spring training now too much of a chore?" the interviewer queried.

"Well, you know I never have been eager for the March work." Giuseppe replied. "However, I make the best of it. Once I get started, I work hard, and get myself in the best possible shape."

"When you reported to Joe McCarthy at St. Petersburg in March, 1936, did you figure you would last this long?"

"I never gave the duration of my Yankee career any thought then, because I was intent on making good," DiMaggio said.

"I want to pay tribute to Bill Essick. The Yankee scout who just has retired," DiMaggio went on.

"He, and he alone, scouted me. He was the only major league agent who had the sense to take me to a surgeon and find out about my knee, which all the others were so sure would disqualify me from a major career. Essick told Ed Barrow to buy me. Remember, the price was $25,000 and a few players. Was I a bargain?"

Has Many Propositions, Nothing Definite Planned

"If this should be your final season, what would you turn to?" Joe was asked.

"I have a lot of propositions," DiMaggio replied. "But I have nothing definite in mind at this time. Radio and television? I don't know. When the time comes, I will make my decision. There is no rush. Remember, I have another season before me. I haven't quit yet."

"What are the Yankees going to do when you hang them up, Joe?"

"Oh, they will go on winning for many years to come," DiMaggio exclaimed. "The club has a great system. It has a lot of very impressive kids right now. I did not see the 25 farm hands who worked out here for a couple of weeks. But I am told that most were really outstanding."

Giuseppe then talked about the 19-year-old Mickey Mantle, whom Casey Stengel is converting into an outfielder, and who may turn out to be DiMaggio's successor.

"Casey has not asked me to help instruct Mantle, but if he is in Tommy Henrich's hands, the boy needs no other tutor," the Clipper said. "Tommy is the best possible teacher for the kid."

DiMaggio was suffering from a head cold, but otherwise was in fine shape. His eye was bright, and he looked impressive off the field, as he had at Municipal Stadium. The Yankee Clipper outfitting for the last voyage.

FISHING

FISHING FOR MARLIN AND DETERMINING THE SIZE
OF A RECORD CATCH

The sportsman's attitude toward the marlin differs greatly from that of the commercial fisherman's or the marine biologist's. All three groups of people, however, are interested in documenting the size of the fish. The excerpts below indicate the effort that has gone into documenting the size of record-making catches of marlin. Mrs. Oliver C. Grinnell and many others, including Ernest Hemingway himself, contributed to *American Big Game Fishing*, in a first-of-a-kind effort to systematize that sport. Grinnell's introduction to that work and charts provided later in the book explain that the records in the mid-1930s—the period during which Hemingway began big-game fishing and when he observed the Cuban fisherman who had been towed for two days by a giant marlin—were at best incomplete on the subject of size. Grinnell's introduction affirms a growing interest in fishing for marlin. Her description of fishing for big game also contains many elements found in *The Old Man and the Sea*—the beauty of the ocean and the marine life, in particular. It is significant that Santiago makes his living with a fish others seek for sport, but clearly, his estimates of the marlin's weight and size are, at best, inexact or perhaps exaggerated.

The second excerpt, from an article by Captain Rick Gaffney in *Marlin*, describes the record catch of a black marlin by Alfred Glassell, a record that stands even today at 1,560 pounds. Interestingly, Glassell caught his marlin just a year after the publication of *The Old Man and the Sea*. As the article reveals, statistics on record catches of marlin were very much in the news as Hemingway was composing his novella.

FROM MRS. OLIVER C. GRINNELL, "INTRODUCTION" AND
"WORLD RECORDS"

(*In American Big Game Fishing*, ed. Eugene V. Connett; New York:
Derrydale Press, 1935)

Big game fishing has at last come into its own. While a few scattered
sportsmen have angled for a quarter of a century for big game fish there
have been less than a hundred who have fished seriously as a major sport
until the last five years.

Big game fishing is destined, and rightly so, to become one of the
greatest, if not the greatest sport of all nations. Originating mainly on the
Pacific Coast for tuna and swordfish and on the Florida coast for tarpon,
today sportsmen are following the game fish wherever they migrate and
records are being made at points heretofore unknown as sources for
sport fishing.

It is not merely *fishing* that attracts our men and women to this grand
sport—environment plays a mighty part. No other sport offers such pan-
orama of beauty, never twice alike. Each day out there on the ocean is
different from its predecessor. Some days are so calm that seaweed floats
in masses and the submerged reefs are visible. On such days it seems as
though the wheeling of the gulls and the flight of the man-of-war birds
is lazy and slow, fitting in with the glassy sea. On other days, the waves
are choppy-bright and white with foam. Your boat dances up and down
and sidewise all at once. Then there are times when sudden squalls
darken the skies, sunshine and shadows intermingle to produce kalei-
doscopic effects of seascape that are surpassingly gorgeous. Often from
these blue waters one may be fortunate in seeing a school of flying fish
rise, bits of shining silver gliding through the air a hundred feet, their
brilliant bodies glistening in the sun. No money could buy a framed paint-
ing half as beautiful.

Then there is always the fresh, stinging, tangy, salty air; the vastness
and beauty of ever-changing blue waters, the indescribable sunrises and
sunsets, the meeting of the sky and the water on the horizon, the intan-
gible something that levels the problems of life, that makes real men and
real women, that puts deep sea anglers in a class by themselves; and I
predict that the devotees will in time be as vast as the sea itself.

There is nothing in history to tell us just when and how a rod, a line
and a hook were used for the first time to catch either fresh or salt water
fish.

Whoever first opened up the sport of deep sea fishing should have a
great and lasting monument dedicated to him, for he gave to thousands

recreation and pleasure that grows and will continue to grow as the years go by.

He of faint heart should not take up the sport of big game fishing, for the taking of large and stubborn sea monsters presents thrills and problems that call for good generalship and a hefty brand of stick-to-it-iveness on the part of the enthusiast who is handling the rod. It takes patience, for days upon days are sometimes passed without even sighting one of these prized fish. Generally speaking, big game angling should never be taken up where backbone and grit are lacking. (xiii–xiv)

• • •

Today marlin have become an important factor in the angling world. They appear to be more plentiful than swordfish and while the majority weigh in the neighborhood of a hundred pounds, large specimens are encountered on occasion.

At Bimini, a British Island, 45 miles east of Miami, during certain seasons of the year, marlin of prodigious size—some of them estimated at 1000 to 1200 pounds, have been sighted. Large specimens are found off New Zealand, various points in the South Seas, and Tahiti Island, where "Carrie Fin" (Mrs. Eastham Guild) landed a monster specimen weighing 856 pounds. Because of the close proximity of Bimini Island to Miami it is to be expected that some worth while records will be made there.

The first marlin to be taken on rod and reel of which we have record was one taken in 1903 by Edward Llewellyn of Los Angeles; while the first one to be taken in the North Atlantic was taken by Julian Crandall off Block Island.

There has been much discussion as to how many varieties of marlin are known. The marlin has erroneously been referred to as a swordfish. The marlin does not belong to the swordfish family but to the spearfish family and it is generally conceded there are at least four varieties; the black marlin, the blue marlin, the striped marlin and the common or white marlin.

The differences in opinion on every variety of salt water fish force upon us the realization of the crying necessity for more research and study— their habits, their feeding and breeding places and where they migrate, as all our pelagic fishes are known to do. Again, we have no authentic record and no real knowledge is available of the origin or habits of this grand game fish.

Marlin are surface feeding fish and are perhaps the most spectacular of all our game fishes. When hooked, their leaps, their tail-walking on the surface of the water, their runs at prodigious speed, give the angler who is fortunate enough to hook one of these beauties, a thrill that will forever linger in his angling memories. (xix–xx)

WORLD'S RECORDS

Heaviest Big Game Fish Of Various Species (Over 100 Pounds) Caught With Rod and Reel.

Corrected to April 1, 1935 — Copyright 1935, *Outdoor Life.*

Species	Weight and Year		Angler	Where Caught	Locality
SWORDFISH (Broadbill)	837½ lbs.	1934	W. E. S. Tuker	Chili	Off Tocopilla
MARLIN (Black)	976 lbs.	1926	Laurie D. Mitchell	New Zealand	Bay of Islands
MARLIN (Striped)	692 lbs.	1931	Alfonse Hamann	California	Off Balboa
MARLIN (Blue)	*				
MARLIN (White)	*				
SAILFISH (Pacific)	180 lbs.	1931	William B. Gray	Panama	Gulf of Panama
SAILFISH (Atlantic)	106 lbs.	1929	W. A. Bonnell	Florida	Off Miami Beach
TUNA (Blue Fin)	851 lbs.	1933	L. Mitchell-Henry	England	Off Whitby
TUNA (Allison)	*				
TARPON	232 lbs.	1911	W. A. McLaren	Mexico	Panuco River
WAHOO	124¾ lbs.	1935	J. B. Stickney	Hawaii	Off Oahu
MAKO	798 lbs.	1931	H. White-Wickham	New Zealand	Bay of Islands
YELLOWTAIL	111 lbs.	1926	Zane Grey	New Zealand	Bay of Islands

The earlier records on this chart are taken from the list of records compiled by Van Campen Heilner of *Field & Stream* and Francesca R. La Monte of the American Museum of Natural History.

* Confusion of species and failure to file complete data leave records open.

• • •

No fish are considered eligible for records unless unmutilated, witnessed and taken by angler unaided on rod and reel and according to tackle specifications and accepted angling club rules and practices of the locality where caught. (236)

• • •

No mutilated fish accepted and proof of ethics required before acceptance. (237)

UNITED STATES BIG GAME FISH RECORDS
(Including U. S. Island Possessions.)

Heaviest fish of all recognized game species caught on rod and reel.

Corrected to April 1, 1935 — Copyright 1935, *Outdoor Life.*

Species	Weight and Year		Angler	Where Caught
ALBACORE	64 lbs. 4 ozs.	1912	Frank Kelly	Catalina, Cal.
AMBERJACK	95 lbs.	1916	S. W. Eccles	Long Key, Fla.
BASS (Channel)	74 lbs.	1929	Chas. D. Beckmann	Chincoteague, Va.
BASS (Striped)	73 lbs.	1913	Chas. B. Church	Vineyard Sound, Mass.
BASS (White Sea)	60 lbs.	1904	C. H. Harding	Catalina, Cal.
BLUEFISH	25 lbs.	1874	L. Hathaway	Cohasset, Mass.
BONEFISH	*			
BONITO	*			
DOLPHIN	*			
KINGFISH (Florida)	58 lbs.	1927	May Haines	Long Key, Fla.
MARLIN (Black)	*			
MARLIN (Blue)	*			
MARLIN (Striped)	692 lbs.	1931	Alfonse Hamann	Balboa, Cal.
MARLIN (White)	*			
POLLOCK	*			
SAILFISH (Pacific)				
SAILFISH (Atlantic)	106 lbs.		W. A. Bonnell	Miami, Fla.
SWORDFISH (Atlantic)	505 lbs.		A. Rex Flinn	Montauk Point, N. Y.
SWORDFISH (Pacific)	573 lbs.		Geo. C. Thomas, III	Catalina, Cal.
TARPON	*			
TUNA (Allison)	*			
TUNA (Blue Fin)	705 lbs.		Francis H. Low	New York, N. Y.
WAHOO	124 lbs. 12 ozs.	1935	J. B. Stickney	Honolulu, Hawaii
WEAKFISH	17 lbs. 3 ozs.	1933	F. J. Conzen	Peconic Bay, N. Y.

The earlier records on this chart are taken from the list of records compiled by Van Campen Heilner of *Field & Stream* and Francesca R. La Monte of the American Museum of Natural History.

* Proof of records lacking and/or angler's failure to substantiate claims.

FROM CAPTAIN RICK GAFFNEY, "ALFRED GLASSELL'S LEGACY TO BILLFISHING TRANSCENDS HIS 1,560-POUND BLACK MARLIN WORLD RECORD"

(Marlin [January 1998])

Alfred Glassell's colossal 1,560-pound black marlin, captured August 4, 1953, off Cabo Blanco, Peru, is both the all-tackle and 130-pound-class record for the species, and it remains the ultimate measure of the sport for every serious big marlin fisherman. Unbroken for over 44 years, it remains the longest standing record for any of the marlin species in the International Game Fish Association [IGFA] world record book.

Although Glassell once rode the high tide of worldwide prominence in the sport—culminating in a *Sports Illustrated* cover and feature in the 1950s—few of today's billfishermen know much about him, despite the fact that his name, and that one accomplishment, are legendary in the sport. Yet Glassell has done much more than capture the heaviest marlin ever landed on sport-fishing tackle under IGFA rules.

For instance, Glassell was also the first to boat a black marlin over 1,000 pounds in weight, breaking Capt. Laurie Mitchell's record for a 976-pound black immortalized by Zane Grey in his book, *Tales of an Angler's El Dorado*. Glassell first topped the elusive 1,000-pound mark with a 1,025-pound black marlin he caught off Cabo Blanco, Peru, in April 1952.

Glassell's new record catch was topped within days by Tom Bates, who caught a 1,060-pound black in the same waters. Undaunted, Glassell returned to the waters off Cabo Blanco and pushed the record up to 1,090 pounds that same month. He had set and regained the world record in less than a month with two marlin of better than 1,000 pounds in weight.

The dogged determination that led to that flurry of records began when Glassell first went to New Zealand to try to beat Mitchell's record. He found black marlin in excess of 600 pounds there, but none big enough, so he went back to the drawing board—or chart table as it were. In searching the atlas for an optimum place to fulfill his fantasy, he noted the extraordinary confluence of major oceanic currents that met off Cabo Blanco and resolved to determine if the bait-rich waters there could deliver his quarry.

In May 1951, S. Kip Farrington, one of America's best known saltwater fishermen of the day, organized the Cabo Blanco Club, an exclusive fishing fraternity with a $10,000 membership fee and a somewhat elusive basis for membership selection. The small group of select members had access to club facilities, which included accommodations, dining and lounge areas, and tackle storage and repair facilities. Perhaps most important, the members also had the use of three "motor cruisers" imported from the productive bluefin tuna fishing grounds off Nova Scotia.

Glassell was an early member of the Cabo Blanco Club and in April 1952 was able to realize his dream of topping Mitchell's long-standing record. In the process, he also raised the standard of achievement for every serious marlin fisherman in the world.

Glassell's flurry of record activity that April was somewhat overshadowed when Farrington upped the ante to 1,135 pounds in September 1952. Then Tom Bates again took back the record with a 1,352-pound black, pushing the envelope dramatically. Fortified with the knowledge that commercial fishermen had landed black marlin in the area weighing more than 1,500 pounds. Glassell accepted the challenge. On August 4, 1953, he boated the 1,560-pound record fish that would withstand the test of nearly a half-century of tackle and game-boat improvements[.] . . . (48)

• • •

Of course, Glassell's immense philanthropy to the world of marine science also provided many great fishing opportunities for the man who remembers being pulled off the dock into Caddo Lake by the first fish he ever hooked, back when he was about 4 years old.

He was born on Cuba Plantation in the northwest corner of Louisiana in 1913, the son and grandson of great sportsmen of the Southern tradition who introduced the young man to hunting and fishing at a very early age. By the time he graduated from Louisiana State University he was actively pursuing tarpon and sailfish off Port Aransas, Texas, having had a yen for salt water for as long as he can remember.

Glassell fished the waters of the Gulf of Mexico extensively from the east coast of Mexico around to the west coast of Florida, and in the Atlantic through the Bahamas, up the east coast of Florida and as far north as Nova Scotia, where he fished as a member of the U.S. tuna team for seven years, leading the team as captain one year. His lifetime catches include blue marlin, black marlin, swordfish and bluefin tuna over 600 pounds in weight. . . .

In a time when air transportation was leisurely, accommodations in many places were rudimentary, and access to adequate game boats in most places was minimal, Glassell fished the waters of the world like few before him and few since. Perhaps only those who have been able to mount mother-ship operations in recent years have come close to fishing as many inaccessible fishing spots in the world's oceans as Glassell has.

His legacy includes the largest marlin of any species in the IGFA world record book, an unprecedented series of grander captures in a very short period of time, serious exploration of much of the world's billfish waters and contributions to marine science that will last long after his lifetime.

Glassell is a sportsman, an adventurer, an amateur oceanographer and marine biologist, a philanthropist, a patron of the arts and, truly, a legend in his own time. (51)

RULES GOVERNING FAIR CATCH

In 1936, the Bahamas Marlin and Tuna Club was founded and established rules for catching fish in the Bahamian waters. Ernest

Hemingway was a founding member of this club. Notice that ten rules are established, many of which apply to the manner in which Santiago catches his marlin and attempts to fend off the shark.

FROM RAY TRULLINGER, "NEW BIG FISH CLUB IS ORGANIZED, BUT IT'S AWFULLY HARD TO CRASH"

(*New York City World Telegram*, 23 November 1936)

Another new big fish anglers' association, the Bahamas Marlin and Tuna Club, has just bloomed in our midst, and, judging from the eligibility requirements, it doesn't appear the Membership Committee ever will be snowed under with applications.

To begin with only fish taken from Bahaman [*sic*] waters will qualify the applicant for membership in this rarefied piscatorial company, and it's no secret that the chap who dangles a cut bait in the vicinity of Bimini or Cat Cay must have something more in the old sock than a hole. That alone excludes 99 per cent of the fraternity, but there's another catch, both for men and women aspirants. The former must have taken a tuna, marlin or mako shark (Maw, that mako's here again!) weighing 400 pounds or more, on club specification tackle, and the latter a 300-pound fish, in the same manner.

Considering the fact that no one of any authority has proven the mako shark an inhabitant of the Atlantic Ocean, and that some of our best known big game fishermen have considerable difficulty distinguishing the more common varieties of sharks, it would appear that any sharp-snouted fish would serve admission requirements in the event a marlin or tuna failed to oblige.

While tackle specifications of the new club are still under consideration, angling regulations have been adopted as follows:

1. All fish must be hooked, fought and brought to gaff by the angler, unaided.

2. Aid will refer not only to the angler but to any part of the boat or chair except the rod socket and harness.

3. The fish will be considered brought to gaff when the leader can be reached by the boatman.

4. The boatman may touch no part of the tackle except the leader, but he may adjust or replace the harness during the fight.

5. When brought to gaff a marlin or tuna may be subdued only with a club.

6. A mako shark is considered a game fish and should be gaffed or tail-roped. A mako may not be killed by any means other than a club.

7. The gaff may not have more than twenty feet of rope attached.

8. The rod or reel may not be fastened to the chair during the fight.

9. A reel falling off the rod butt, as well as a broken rod, will disqualify the fish.

10. No mutilated fish will qualify or be considered a legitimate catch.

Officers of the new club include Ernest Hemingway, president; Michael Lerner, Thomas Shevlin and A. O. H. Baldridge, vice presidents; Julio Sanchez, treasurer; S. Kip Farrington, secretary, and Erl Roman, historian.

TOPICS FOR WRITTEN OR ORAL EXPLORATION

1. Perform a numerical inventory of events and facts in *The Old Man and the Sea*. Consider the number of days Santiago has been without a catch, the number of sharks that strike, the number of days Santiago spends at sea. Do these numerical values have any correspondence with significant numbers in baseball generally and with the specific baseball information alluded to in *The Old Man and the Sea*? What might these correspondences suggest, if anything, about the theme of the novella?

2. The bullfighter's demeanor is the epitome of the Hemingway hero's "grace under pressure," undoubtedly a reason that the author became so fond of bullfighting. Hemingway wrote a book about bullfighting, *Death in the Afternoon*, in 1932. Read this book and write an essay in which you compare and contrast elements of bullfighting with those of baseball. Consider such elements as the shape of the baseball field/bullring, the solo performances of the hitter/matador, and so on.

3. Research the contributions of Cubans to major-league baseball in the United States.

4. Write an essay in which you compare and contrast elements in the lives of Santiago and Joe DiMaggio. Use material in this chapter as well as evidence from *The Old Man and the Sea*. Focus on topics such as the hardships and pain each must endure in pursuit of their goals, their common background as sons of poor fishermen, and the like. Conclude your essay with a determination about whether the similarities or the differences between these men are greater.

5. Both DiMaggio and Santiago came from humble origins. Write a journal entry in which you reflect upon how and why the real-life baseball player and the fictional character end up very differently.

6. Santiago and Manolin admire ballplayers who have had to overcome some adversity or difficulty in order to succeed. Write an essay in which you explain the adversities each ballplayer mentioned in the novella had to overcome and why these particular difficulties would provide inspiration to the Cuban fishermen.

7. Compare Santiago's remarks on fishing with his comments on baseball, specifically his remarks about DiMaggio. Write an essay in which you compare and contrast baseball and fishing. In what ways would *The Old Man and the Sea* lead the reader to believe that fishing and playing baseball are similar?

8. Santiago/Manolin, George Sisler/Dick Sisler, Joe DiMaggio/Mickey Mantle: Each pair contains an older man, role model, father figure

and a younger man, aspiring professional, son figure. Write a journal entry, using information about these men from this chapter and the novella, from one of the following perspectives:

- The Older Man: How does he feel about the younger man? Does the younger man represent a threat, a rival, or a person to pick up where the older man has left off? Does the older man want the younger one to succeed professionally, or does the older man secretly hope that he remains the undisputed master of his profession?

- The Younger Man: How does he feel about the older man? Is the older man seen as a mentor or a daunting figure, one whose accomplishments can never be surpassed? Does the relationship with the older man inspire the younger one to achievements or intimidate him into an inferior position? In your response, consider how these associations differ when the men are related by blood.

9. Santiago makes many comments about fishing, and his actions supply another source of information about how one should fish. Using techniques and advice derived from Santiago's remarks, write a process essay in which you give advice on how to fish.

10. Both Santiago and Alfred Glassell are fishermen—one a professional, the other a sportsman. In an essay, compare and contrast these men and their achievements as fishermen. Make the thesis of this essay your claim that either the differences or the similarities between them are more significant.

11. Lillian Ross, the author of a book titled *Portrait of Hemingway*, said that Ernest Hemingway did not consider his age to be old at the time of her interview with him. Ross quotes Hemingway as saying: " 'It is sort of fun to be fifty and feel you are going to defend the title again,' he said. 'I won it in the twenties and defended it in the thirties and the forties, and I don't mind at all defending it in the fifties' " (46). Apply this sentiment to Santiago. Does he successfully defend his title?

12. You may have heard the saying "Success is 1 percent inspiration and 99 percent perspiration." Apply this idea to *The Old Man and the Sea*. Both Santiago and DiMaggio have enormous natural talent for what they undertake; they both have enormous experience and practice in their fields. Write a journal entry in which you reflect upon the relative importance of natural talent as something distinct from experience and practice as causes of an individual's success in a chosen field.

13. Both Santiago and DiMaggio have "streaks": eighty-five days without a catch for the fisherman; fifty-six consecutive games with hits for the ballplayer. Write a journal entry in which you discuss how the repeated successes, or the lack of them, affect an individual's performance. Do people have good or bad luck, or do people make good or bad luck for themselves?

14. In a journal entry, write about a situation in which you have persisted in your efforts to attain a goal despite great physical pain or other discomfort. What were the results? How did you feel about your ability to persevere? Or perhaps you did not persevere and allowed pain or discomfort or difficulty to prevent your accomplishment of a goal. How did you feel about this? What have you learned from Santiago or Joe DiMaggio about overcoming difficulty in pursuit of a goal?

15. Age need not be a barrier to success. Write an essay in which you reflect upon elderly people you have known and their contributions to professions or volunteer organizations.

16. Using evidence from *The Old Man and the Sea*, write an essay in which your thesis is that Santiago can be compared to an athlete in training.

17. Risk-taking is an aspect of both Santiago's character and Durocher's. Debate the ways in which these men took risks. Were the risks worthwhile, or did these men at times take risks that did not pay off?

SUGGESTED READINGS AND WORKS CITED

"Arm Wrestling." *Encyclopedia of World Sport: From Ancient Times to the Present* Vol. 1. Ed. David Levinson and Karen Christensen. Santa Barbara: ABC-CLIO, 1996.

"Arm Wrestling History." At www.armwrestling.com/history/html; accessed 14 June 2001.

Bjarkman, Peter C. "First Hispanic Star? Dolf Luque, of Course." *Baseball Research Journal* 19 (1990): 28–32.

Complete Baseball. CD-ROM. Microsoft Corporation, 1994.

Cramer, Richard Ben. *Joe DiMaggio: The Hero's Life*. New York: Simon & Schuster, 2000.

"Cuban Winter Baseball League." Clipping file. Cooperstown, NY: National Baseball Hall of Fame, 1949.

Dewey, Donald, and Nicholas Acocella, eds. *The Biographical History of Baseball*. New York: Carroll & Graf Publishers, 1995.

"DiMaggio, Joe." *Microsoft Encarta Online Encyclopedia*. 2001 ed. At http://www.encarta.msn.com; © 1997–2001, Microsoft Corporation.

Eskenazi, Gerald. *The Lip: A Biography of Leo Durocher*. New York: William Morrow, 1993.

González Echevarría, Roberto. *The Pride of Havana: A History of Cuban Baseball*. New York: Oxford University Press, 1999.

Graham, Frank. *McGraw of the Giants*. New York: G.P. Putnam's Sons, 1944.

Hemingway, Ernest. *Death in the Afternoon*. New York: Charles Scribner's Sons, 1932.

———. "Hemingway on Mutilated Fish." *Outdoor Life* 77 (June 1936): 70–72.

———. "Marlin Off the Cost of Morro: A Cuban Letter." *Esquire* 1:1 (Autumn 1933): 8, 39, 97. Reprint, Ernest Hemingway, *By-Line: Ernest Hemingway*, ed. William White (New York: Touchstone, 1967), 137–43.

Hurley, C. Harold, ed. *Hemingway's Debt to Baseball in* The Old Man and the Sea*: A Collection of Critical Readings*. Lewiston, NY: Edwin Mellen Press, 1992; see particularly in this volume: Samuel E. Longmire's "Hemingway's Praise of Dick Sisler in *The Old Man and the Sea*" (9–11); George Monteiro's "Santiago, DiMaggio, and Hemingway: The Ageing Professionals of *The Old Man and the Sea*" (29–38); and Hurley's own "The Facts Behind the Fiction: The 1950 American League Pennant Race" (77–93) and "Just a 'Boy' or 'Already a Man'? Manolin's Age in *The Old Man and the Sea*" (95–101).

Jamail, Milton H. *Full Count: Inside Cuban Baseball*. Carbondale: Southern Illinois University Press, 2000.

Obituary, Mike Gonzalez clipping file, April 2, 1977. Cooperstown, NY: National Baseball Hall of Fame.

Pérez, Louis A., Jr. "Between Baseball and Bullfighting: The Quest for Nationality in Cuba, 1868–1898." *Journal of American History* (September 1994): 493–517.

———. *On Becoming Cuban: Identity, Nationality, and Culture*. Chapel Hill: University of North Carolina Press, 1999.

Pietrusza, David. *Top Ten Baseball Managers*. Springfield, NJ: Enslow Publishers, 1999.

Plath, James. "Santiago at the Plate: Baseball and *The Old Man and the Sea*." *Hemingway Review* 16:1 (Fall 1996): 65–88.

Ross, Lillian. *Portrait of Hemingway*. New York: Simon & Schuster, 1961.

Rucker, Mark, and Peter C. Bjarkman. *Smoke: The Romance and Lore of Cuban Baseball*. New York: Sports Illustrated, 1999.

Schoor, Gene. *The Leo Durocher Story*. New York: Messer, 1955.

Seidel, Michael. *Streak: Joe DiMaggio and the Summer of '41*. New York: Penguin, 1989.

Spoto, Donald. *Marilyn Monroe: The Biography*. New York: Harper-Collins, 1993.

Stein, Fred. "John Joseph McGraw." In *Biographical Dictionary of American Sports: Baseball*, ed. David L. Porter. Westport, CT: Greenwood Press, 1987.

"United States Armsport." At www.armwrestling.com, accessed 14 June 2001.

Ward, J. J. "Gonzales [*sic*], the Cuban Backstop." *Baseball Magazine* (February 1917): 33–34.

6

The Old Man and the Sea: Contemporary Issues

The Old Man and the Sea was set in the Cuba that Ernest Hemingway knew—that is, Cuba of the late 1940s and early 1950s. This setting liberally incorporates the specific elements of Cuban geography that were discussed in Chapter 2. Although the island's natural resources may have been depleted over the last half century, Cuba's climate, coastal waters, and the marine organisms in those waters remain unchanged thus far in the twenty-first century.

The novella also reflects Hemingway's experience of Cuban history and ethnicity, the topics discussed in Chapters 3 and 4, respectively. But several years after the publication of *The Old Man and the Sea*, the history of the Cuban people took a dramatic turn when Fidel Castro and his revolutionary government imposed a Communist regime on that island nation. Clearly, had Hemingway set *The Old Man and the Sea* in the Cuba of the late twentieth or the early twenty-first century, the political atmosphere reflected in his novella—and the details of setting, character, and plot dictated by that atmosphere—would have affected Santiago's portrayal as a Roman Catholic man who seeks his living as a private fisherman.

Finally, sport—specifically the sport of baseball, the topic examined in Chapter 5—presents an interesting constant in Cuban experience. Indeed, the allusions to baseball players, teams, and play-off games constitute the most specific identification of real-world events outside the novella. Although the players, teams, and games would be different were *The Old Man and the Sea* set in the twenty-first century, baseball itself could remain an important element in the novella's setting and in its development of character. Notwithstanding Cuba's official repudiation of most things associated with the United States, Cubans continue to enjoy baseball as their major sporting pastime.

HISTORY: POLITICS AND ECONOMICS UNDER CASTRO

Fidel Castro and his insurgents began changing the political and social climate of Cuba during the late 1950s (see Chapter 3). Ernest Hemingway, among others, became increasingly aware of the violence caused by Castro's guerrilla warfare surrounding him at Finca Vigía. When Hemingway realized that prudence dictated his departure from Cuba, he and his wife, Mary, left for Ketchum, Idaho.

On 1 January 1959, Fidel Castro succeeded in taking over the Cuban government of Fulgencia Batista in a coup. Many Americans hoped that this new regime spelled the end of dictatorship and economic oppression in Cuba. Sharing that optimism, the Hemingways returned to Cuba at the end of 1959. Although Finca Vigía had sustained some damage during their absence, Mary Hemingway praised Castro's efforts and reforms at the time (Reynolds 334). Ernest Hemingway demonstrated his approval of Castro's regime by kissing the hem of the Cuban flag upon landing in Cuba. Although Hemingway met Castro only once, their meeting was cordial because it involved Hemingway's favorite pastime—fishing; on 15 May 1960, Castro won the individual fishing championship in the Hemingway Tournament (Fuentes 113).

When Hemingway left Cuba again in June 1960, he feared that he would never return. By then, he had descended into the abyss of profound clinical depression, for which he was treated at the Mayo Clinic in Rochester, Minnesota. Unfortunately, these treatments were not successful, the depression persisted, and on 2 July 1961, Hemingway ended his own life. Even had Hemingway lived, he might never have returned to Cuba because of subsequent events in U.S.-Cuban relations. Few could have guessed that Castro would persist as Cuba's leader into the twenty-first century, remaining the only Communist head of state in the Western Hemisphere and one of the only Communist leaders left in the world.

Almost immediately after his revolutionary coup in 1959, Castro became prime minister of Cuba, a position he maintained until 1976. He then assumed the role of president and remains as such as of this writing. Within months of Castro's coming to power, numerous associates of Batista who had not fled the island were executed, and U.S. relations with the new Cuban government deteriorated quickly. Castro's government appropriated American properties as part of the elimination of all private property in Cuba and declared Cuba to be an atheist country. Both the elimination of private property and the imposition of atheism were part of Castro's Communist agenda.

Communism is an ideology first articulated by Karl Marx and Friedrich Engels in *The Communist Manifesto*, published in 1848. Believing that capitalism would engender eternal strife between worker and employer—that is, between the bourgeoisie and the proletariat—Marx and Engels called for the elimination of all private property. Communal ownership of all the resources and means of production evolved as the goal of the Communist economy. "From each, according to his abilities, to each, according to his needs" became one of the many slogans associated with communism. Thus, theoretically, both the street cleaner and the doctor would be equally assured the essentials needed to live, and each would be required to contribute to society according to his gifts. A classless society would be the result of this economic system.

Marx also believed that one of the reasons members the proletariat failed to revolt against their oppressors was because institutionalized religion conspired to keep workers from realizing the full misery of their oppression. Another slogan associated with Marxist communism, "Religion is the opium of the people," signifies that religion dulls the pain of poverty and injustice with claims of rewards in the hereafter. Consequently, Castro's imposition of communism upon Cuba brought with it repression of institutionalized religion and altered a specific aspect of Cuban ethnic experience, the practice of Roman Catholicism.

The imposition of an ideology so at odds with the beliefs of both Cuban exiles and official U.S. policy soon led to military tensions. Two years after Castro came to power, a group of Cuban exiles attempted to mount an insurrection. In April 1961, these exiles invaded Cuba at the Baya de los Cochinos (the Bay of Pigs). The United States had supported this effort, but the invasion was a terrible failure, a gross miscalculation of the popular support Castro had garnered among his people.

Relations between the two countries reached their nadir in October 1962 in what has come to be known as the "Cuban Missile Crisis." U.S. reconnaissance planes detected the presence of Soviet missiles in Cuba; many in the United States believed that the country was on the brink of nuclear war. President John F. Kennedy engaged in negotiations with Soviet Premier Nikita Khrushchev, which culminated in the United States' agreeing not to invade Cuba in exchange for Khrushchev's agreeing to remove the missiles from the island. Following the Cuban Missile Crisis, the United States prohibited its citizens' traveling to Cuba and instituted an economic embargo, which prohibited U.S. companies from engaging in any financial or commercial transactions with that island country.

The U.S. measures aimed at forcing Cubans to abandon their association with the Soviets were as much a failure as the Bay of Pigs invasion. Castro continued to embrace communism overtly and came to rely (partially because of U.S. policy) on the Soviet Union for economic as well as military aid. Castro also attempted to bring other Latin American countries into the Soviet fold and supported revolutionary movements in South and Central America, as well as in Africa, deploying thousands of Cuban troops to Ethiopia in the late 1970s.

Many Cuban citizens found living under Castro's Communist regime so oppressive that they risked their lives to flee Cuba. Starting in the 1960s, in makeshift boats sometimes no larger than Santiago's fishing skiff, thousands upon thousands of Cubans sought freedom in the United States by sailing across the Straits of Florida and the Gulf of Mexico. With the demise of the Soviet Union at the beginning of the 1990s and the continuing U.S. blockade of essential goods into Cuba, the economic situation of the average Cuban deteriorated to the point that many Cubans began to flee their island for financial as well as ideological reasons. Numerous Cubans died in these attempts.

Others who arrived in Florida became embroiled in immigration and political struggles. One such case was that of Elian Gonzales, the six-year-old lone survivor of a group of Cubans who had sought to flee their island in a small motorboat. Elian was picked up floating in an inner tube off the Florida shore on Thanksgiving Day in 1999. His father had remained in Cuba, but his mother had died in her attempt to reach the United States. Elian was placed with relatives in Miami and thereby became the focus of an international custody and immigration battle that ended in April 2000, when U.S. immigration officials forcibly removed him from his relatives' custody in Miami and returned him to his father.

After more than four decades of Castro's rule, world opinion is sharply divided about whether the life of the average Cuban citizen is better or worse than it was under Batista. Would the life of a man such as Santiago have been improved if Hemingway had depicted such a person as a citizen under the Communist Castro government? The two men who may have been prototypes for Santiago have answered this question very differently. The fisherman Anselmo Hernandez was among the thousands of Cubans who judged Castro's regime to be so noxious that they risked their lives to flee it. In 1965, at the age of ninety-two, Hernandez was among 250 persons who fled Cuba by crossing the Straits of Florida in small boats. However, the fisherman and captain of Hemingway's pleasure boat, Gregorio Fuentes (who is depicted in the illustration in Chapter 2), stayed in Cuba. A picture of Fuentes appeared in the March 2000 issue of *Vanity Fair* in an article on the persistent charms of Havana. Fuentes was 102 years of age when his photograph was taken. As a very old man, he augmented his income during the Castro era by giving paid interviews about his life and experiences with Ernest Hemingway.

That Fuentes had to augment his income thus bespeaks the poverty that still plagues the average Cuban. Fuentes's actions also demonstrated that many Cubans seek entrepreneurial, essentially capitalistic means (in his case, with the occasional tourist) to survive in today's Cuba. But the tourist industry is very different in today's Cuba than it was during the Batista regime. American tourism, then a major contributor to the Cuban economy, has not been legal in more than forty years, although in the past few years, more and more Americans have attempted to take advantage of the island's beauty for pleasure and recreation. Because Americans are prohibited by law from spending money in Cuba, many seek to evade this prohibition and to vacation in Cuba by booking prepaid tours through other countries. Some Americans enter Cuba via the Bahamas, Canada, or Mexico, and Cuban officials conspire with the Americans' illegal entry into their country by not stamping their passports. Although the Clinton administration had demonstrated tolerance toward Americans traveling to Cuba, the Bush administration is much more aggressive about identifying these tourists and slapping them with fines that, while typically $7,500, can be as high as $55,000 (Bruni 9).

It is highly unlikely, therefore, that if *The Old Man and the Sea* were placed in a contemporary setting, it would include Santiago's innocent observation of a plane en route to Miami; nor could the novella conclude with U.S. tourists casually conversing at a seaside restaurant. Any mention of American travel to or presence in Cuba would be fraught with political significance and implications about the tense relationship between the two countries, which have long since ceased diplomatic relations.

Surely, U.S. tourists, if they were found in a restaurant in a contemporary version of *The Old Man and the Sea*, would not find themselves in a restaurant like the Terrace. Restaurants in Cuba have been run by the state since Castro's takeover. These restaurants produce food that is by many standards unsavory; service and ambience are also woefully lacking. But in 1995, in response to the failure of Cuba's Communist economy, the government legalized restaurants in private homes. Known as *paladares*, these restaurants are highly regulated and taxed. To avoid these restrictions, illegally operated private restaurants have emerged. According to *New York Times* food critic Marian Burros, the tourist will find better food in the *paladares* than in the state-run restaurants or the illegal private restaurants that are advertised by word of mouth on the street (8).

Paladares serve cuisine that is still influenced by Cuba's Spanish and African ethnic origins. The dish of black beans and rice continues to be a staple. *Ropa vieja* (which literally means "old clothes") the Cuban meal traditionally made with beef simmered in spices until it falls apart, is now made with lamb in the *paladares* because beef is allowed only in the state-run restaurants. *Chorizo*, Spanish sausage, and *chicharrónes*, fried pork rinds, are other traditional Cuban foods that are still served.

These private restaurants acquire a variety of ambiences based upon the homes in which they are found. Some are located in homes built in the 1950s, others are found in restored colonial buildings. In each case, the *paladares* offer a very different kind of dining experience from that American tourists experienced in pre-Castro Cuba, when they ate in lavish resort casinos or café bars in small coastal fishing villages (Burros 8, 20).

Restaurants were but one aspect of Cuban business that Castro's government attempted to deprivatize. The fishing industry also ceased to be a private industry. According to David Abel, reporting for the *Christian Science Monitor* in 1998, the Office of Fishing Inspections in Havana imposes many requirements upon Cuban fishermen. They must obtain certificates attesting to the safety of their fishing vessels, ostensibly a measure aimed at protecting fishermen at sea; but in reality, the regulation controls the exodus of refugees from Cuba. Fishermen are required to have licenses or else face hefty fines. The bureaucracy involved in obtaining these certificates and licenses prompts many fishermen to evade the entire process and fish illegally. Numerous fishermen, plying their trade without proper equipment such as fishing rods, take to the seas to catch a free meal or to obtain a source of black-market income (Abel 7). Were *The Old Man and the Sea* set in today's Cuba, Santiago would undoubtedly be depicted as a man burdened either by a complex bureaucracy or by the subterfuges needed to fish independent of government regulation.

Would Castro's Communist regime give a man such as Santiago access to better medical attention at the turn of the twentieth century? The answer to this question, like the answers to questions in other areas of life affected by Cuban politics and economics, varies due to the changing circumstances of Castro's regime over the last fifty years. As recently as the summer of 2001, the *New York Times* reported that Castro had offered scholarships to Cuba's Latin American School of Medical Sciences to U.S. citizens. Several accepted Castro's offer not only because it provided them the opportunity to obtain an expensive education for free, but also because under Castro, Cuba had gained a positive reputation for its healthcare system, particularly in areas of preventive and holistic medicine. Under Castro, Cuba was indisputably a leader in medicine among third-world nations, and doctors from Cuba had been sent to many other impoverished countries around the world ("Dreams Lead All the Way to Havana").

But many published reports from various sources counter the

above indication that Cuba is a leader in health care, documenting the tremendous difficulties Cuban citizens experience when they require medical attention. Cuba's reliance on herbal remedies as part of its emphasis on holistic medicine may be less due to medical innovation than a demonstration of chronic shortages in all areas. Cuban doctors must frequently find substitutes for medicines that other countries import from the United States. Patients often rely on black market aspirin to ease their pain after surgery; even soap and sterile dressings are in short supply, as are machines needed to warm blood for transfusions. Doctors and nurses are paid inadequately, and, at times, hospital patients can only obtain a nurse's care if the nurse is paid under the table. Spending on health services, heavily supported by the former Soviet Union, has decreased by 70% since 1989 ("What Ails Cuba's Health Service").

Indeed, both pro- and anti-Castro factions assert that there are huge problems in Cuban health care, but these factions attribute the problems to different causes. The American Association for World Health in its "Summary of Findings" for 1997 asserts that "the U.S. embargo of Cuba has dramatically harmed the health and nutrition of large numbers of Cuban citizens." The AAWH states that the embargo prohibits the importation to Cuba of many medicines produced by American pharmaceutical corporations, thus drastically limiting the number of medicines available to Cuban citizens. Furthermore, the ban on the sale of food produced in the United States also has an adverse affect upon the health of the average Cuban, cutting his or her caloric intake to 33% of what it was in 1989 ("Denial of Food and Medicine: The Impact of the U.S. Embargo on the Health and Nutrition in Cuba").

Official press releases from the U.S. Department of State, however, contradict the assertion that these shortages are attributable to the embargo, citing "the Cuban Democracy Act of 1992 which permits American companies and their subsidiaries to sell medicine and medical equipment to Cuba." Rather, the Department of State implicates a two-tier system of "medical apartheid" that provides state-of-the-art medical services to tourists who pay handsomely for care that is unavailable to the average, impoverished Cuban. Members of the higher echelons of Cuban government and the Communist Party are also able to avail themselves of these finer medical facilities ("The U.S. Embargo and Health Care: Myth Versus

Reality"). It is not the embargo, says the Department of State, but the structure of Cuban society that prevents its average citizen from obtaining adequate health care and nutrition.

If one puts credence in the claims of the Department of State or the American Association for World Health, one may conclude that the nutritional and medical state of a fictional character such as Santiago, created for a contemporary novella, would have to be represented just as he was in *The Old Man and the Sea*. Today's *viejo* would most likely be forced to treat symptoms such as diarrhea, nausea, sun spots, and cramps with his own, home remedies. And he would probably continue to rely on traditional preventive measures such as fortifying himself with shark oil.

ETHNICITY: RELIGIOUS PRACTICE

A hallmark of Santiago's experience as a fisherman in *The Old Man and the Sea* is its utter simplicity. As we have seen, his livelihood in today's Cuba would be characterized by great complexity, a characteristic that would also affect the place of religion in his life. The practice of Roman Catholicism has been suppressed throughout Castro's regime, but religion, like the economy, is an aspect of Cuban life changing once again at the beginning of the new century. During the last decade of the twentieth century, the Cuban government became more tolerant of religion, even permitting a visit to the island by Pope John Paul II. There is an increase in religious observation and practice in Cuba. Nonetheless, the last two generations of Cubans who grew up in an officially Communist, atheist country are not likely to have pictures of the Virgen del Cobre or the Sacred Heart of Jesus hanging on the walls of their homes. A *viejo* such as Santiago would probably have been brought up as a Catholic before the revolution, so the author of such a character would have the option of whether or not to have his or her character utter the prayers that had probably been learned as a child, especially if the setting for this utterance were the privacy of a small boat in the middle of the sea. Similarly, the author would have to decide whether or not to have the Santiago-like protagonist promise to make a pilgrimage in exchange for a favor.

SPORTS

Baseball may be the area in which Cuba and the United States enjoy the happiest associations. Cubans continue to love the American import of baseball, even though several prominent players on the Cuban National Team have defected to play on North American teams in recent years. Clearly, the lure of a multimillion-dollar contract is a strong one for these players.

As the documents that follow demonstrate, baseball can still supply a contemporary writer of fiction with rich material for allusions that sustain a theme of heroism and team spirit. Baseball figures can also serve as role models and inspirations, even if baseball may not enjoy its former stature as the quintessential sport for Americans, as it did in the 1950s. For Cubans, however, baseball continues to occupy a place of premier importance; and if Hemingway were writing *The Old Man and the Sea* today, Santiago and Manolin could still be discussing baseball. Although some present-day Cubans attempt to make a living by fishing and catering to tourists, the following excerpts illustrate how the political climate in contemporary Cuba would force a change in the depiction of both commercial fishing and tourism. Lastly, when the international community thinks about an old man and the sea in relationship to today's Cuba, that old man at sea is probably one who, like Anselmo Hernandez, is risking his life to cross the Straits of Florida in order to reach political freedom in the United States. Certainly, in almost every aspect of plot, setting, and character, a contemporary rendition of *The Old Man and the Sea* would be fraught with political resonances.

THE FISHING, TOURIST, AND RESTAURANT INDUSTRIES IN CUBA DURING CASTRO'S REGIME

The excerpts from a *Los Angeles Times* article below directly address several topics related to this study of the economic and political underpinnings of *The Old Man and the Sea*. Santiago's socioeconomic status as a character was governed by the class to which he belonged during the Batista regime. When Castro came to power, he sought to make all businesses—including the fishing, tourist, and restaurant businesses—more productive and efficient by taking them out of private hands and placing them under the control of the state. How might a fisherman such as Santiago function in today's Cuba? Are tourists still drawn to Cuba, and do they contribute to its economy? In what kind of a restaurant might a tourist eat? Did the changes imposed by Castro's government create more opportunity and a better standard of living for individual Cubans? The reader can use the following excerpts to judge whether this experiment succeeded.

The article that follows begins with an actual allusion to *The Old Man and the Sea* that implies that Santiago would be no less fortunate than a Cuban fisherman of today. Both are forced to forfeit their catches to others. This allusion indicates, moreover, the continuing hold that Hemingway's fictional character has upon the imagination. The second excerpt from the article describes a restaurant where tourists in today's Cuba might eat. Contrast the experience at the *paladares* described below with what the tourists at the end of *The Old Man and the Sea* might have enjoyed at the Terrace.

FROM "MARKET SCENE: CUBANS TASTING CAPITALISM—BUT IT'S JUST AN APPETIZER"

(*Los Angeles Times*, World Report, 29 March 1994)

If an old man of the sea catches a big fish, who gets to keep it? Ernest Hemingway had his old man give it up to the predators of the deep, but in today's Cuba it belongs to Fidel Castro, at least by the rules.

According to the Castro regime's regulations, any fish caught in Cuban waters by Cubans belongs to the government. It cannot be processed or sold privately, even though recent reforms permit private enterprise in a few fields.

The regulations are a matter of great distress to Chincho Calacon, by Cuban standards an old man at 63 but also a man of opportunity.

Calacon is one of a handful of defiant Cubans challenging Castro's rigid economic system, under which nearly everybody works for the state in one way or the other.

His way is, with some friends, to fish illegally for marlin and other large fish from old tractor-tire inner tubes, using only a plastic line and their hands. No poles, no gaffs, no nets.

Unable to get a proper license either to operate a boat or to fish, Calacon and three or four associates have joined the black market, which for dollars—lots of them—will provide almost anything that the Castro regime either can't or won't, at least not at a fair price. . . .

His urge or need to acquire dollars sends Calacon out of Havana Harbor in the black sky before dawn several days a week, towing the oversized inner tubes behind a tiny rowboat powered by a small, sputtering motor.

After an hour [or] so of stomach-churning roller-coasting through the whitecaps of the harbor and into the open sea, Calacon has his associates clamber into the inner tubes and toss out their lines, holding the spools in their leathery hands.

On one recent trip, a young man—Hector, he called himself—got a hit on his line after bobbing about for just under two hours. Very carefully he pulled in the fish, hand over hand on the plastic line.

It was a small marlin, and it was not clubbed or gaffed for fear of attracting sharks that were sensed but not seen in the water. Instead, when the exhausted prey was tugged close, the other men paddled over and helped haul the fish onto Hector's inner tube. He held it against his chest while it suffocated. After another hour, the little armada gathered itself and returned to Havana.

Calacon cut up the fish and began selling the pieces on the Malecon, Havana's bay front. In short order, he sold about 15 pounds of marlin at $3 a pound. U.S. currency only, no exceptions.

The old man['s] last legitimate job was in a bicycle assembly plant now closed for lack of parts[.]

• • •

[K]nown as *paladares* are the most prominent of the little businesses that have sprung up[.] . . . They are popular because they provide food found not even in the expensive restaurants limited to tourists. In addition, the *paladares* are cheap, at least for foreigners with dollars. . . .

The best of the lot, arranged through the help of a government functionary, was in an old mansion in Miramar, the neighborhood that once housed the pre-Castro elite and now serves diplomats, foreign business people and Castro's favored few.

A visitor was brought in through a side garden after an exchange of coded knocks on a gate. The dining table was on a veranda next to a kitchen. The stars above looked three-dimensional, the breeze wafted and the Chopin etudes on the CD player sounded enchanting.

The visitor was in the second of three sittings that night, each given 90 minutes to eat. Before the meal was served, the owner-chef asked for drink orders, apologizing for having only one single-malt Scotch.

"We are not accustomed to a big selection," he said, "but I've put in an order for three more brands. Is there one you would particularly like?"

The menu was limited to one selection arranged in advance by the go-between. This night it was cold asparagus with a hollandaise sauce as an appetizer, a salad of tomatoes and sliced onions, broiled snapper with steamed carrots and baby potatoes. Dessert was a choice of fresh fruit or cake.

A Spanish sparkling wine was offered along with three Spanish still wines. The meal was capped with a choice of five Cuban cigars.

The bill for four people came to $76, U.S. currency, of course.

A grand evening, except. The asparagus was canned and tinny tasting, the onions soggy, the snapper dry and overcooked, the fruit limited to orange slices and the $8 cigar stale. (3:1)

PROTOTYPE FOR *THE OLD MAN AND THE SEA* AS REFUGEE

Old men and the sea: Santiago and Anselmo Hernandez. Hemingway's fictional Cuban fisherman confronted the challenges posed by the sea to his livelihood. So did the real-life Cuban fisherman Anselmo Hernandez; but this man eventually took to the sea for an additional motive—that of fleeing to the United States to seek freedom from his government's oppression. Thus the Straits of Florida with their choppy waters were an adversary for both men, an adversary to be overcome under the scorching sun in small boats with meager provisions. But both *viejos* seemed fearless, armed as they were with enormous courage, apparent disregard for their own safety, and fierce determination to reach their goals. Although Santiago's purpose at sea was his pursuit of a great marlin and the desire to break his streak of bad luck, the reader must decide whether or not he reached these goals during his three-day ordeal. Anselmo Hernandez's motive, as recorded in the *New York Times* article below, was to arrive safely upon the Florida shores, a goal he evidently accomplished. Hernandez, at the age of ninety-two, demonstrated a remarkable capacity for endurance, much like the fictional character he claimed to have inspired.

"CUBANS RESUME THEIR EXODUS BY BOAT ACROSS FLORIDA STRAIT"

(*New York Times*, 22 October 1965)

Fisherman Among Arrivals at Key West Says He Is Model for 'Old Man and Sea'

Key West, Fla., Oct. 21 (AP)—More than 250 Cuban refugees—the largest number since Premier Fidel Castro relaxed the exit ban two weeks ago—crossed the choppy Florida Strait today.

They brought to an end a two-day lull in the exodus from the Communist island. The arrivals reported that a fleet of more than 250 small boats was waiting behind to make the trip.

Among the new exiles was a grizzled, 92-year-old fisherman who said he had inspired Ernest Hemingway's novel, "The Old Man and the Sea."

The 15 small boats crossed the 90-mile stretch of ocean at such a clip today that the Coast Guard, which has been trying to escort every boat into port, could not keep up.

Twenty-seven refugees and three crewmen crowded into a 20-foot motorboat, the Cherokee and made the trip in the sweltering sun. . . .

One boat carrying 54 exiles—the largest single group so far—chugged unescorted into Marathon in the middle of the Florida Keys.

A second, smaller, boat landed at a bathing beach near Key West. Still another put in at a shrimp fleet pier. For a time, the Coast Guard had so many in sight it could not keep track.

The new arrivals brought to more than 800 the number who have fled Cuba since Oct. 10.

Anselmo Hernandez, a spry, wiry fisherman, said he was the model for Hemingway's story of an old man's fight with a great fish in a small boat.

But the author's widow, Mary Hemingway, said in New York that the novel was not about any one person, although Hemingway had known Hernandez well.

"Hemingway and I fished together one entire season," the fisherman said here. "Every time he was in Cuba he came to see me. I was the one Hemingway wrote that book about."

The exodus had stopped early Tuesday and exiles and officials alike speculated that Premier Castro had put a halt to it. But the Cuban Government said the only reason for the slowdown was bad weather off the coast. (20:1)

THE POSSIBILITIES FOR BASEBALL IN A CONTEMPORARY VERSION OF *THE OLD MAN AND THE SEA*

In the following interview, Timothy J. Wiles, director of research at the National Baseball Hall of Fame in Cooperstown, New York, gives us an insight into how baseball might function were Hemingway's novella set at the end of the twentieth or the beginning of the twenty-first century. Mr. Wiles's tackles the larger question of whether or not baseball itself is a sport that could still sustain the allusive and symbolic qualities with which it is endowed in *The Old Man and the Sea*. Note specifically which baseball players might be used to represent the traits of character and leadership Hemingway wished to convey. Note, further, Mr. Wiles's suggestion that the truth about players and their situations is frequently distorted in order to fit idealized notions of our society, those that reflect the best values Americans associate with themselves. He notes that, despite the political tensions between the United States and Cuba during the last half-century, Cubans, like all Latin Americans, constitute an ever-growing group devoted to American big league baseball, a phenomenon that will assure its place in American culture and American fiction.

INTERVIEW WITH TIM WILES

(20 July 2001)

PV: Our purpose in this interview will be to consider how baseball might be presented if Hemingway were writing the book now and setting it today. . . .

TW: Just to give us a starting point: the nature of star players and whether or not they stay with one team, as Joe DiMaggio did during his career.

There's a very common popular perception that that era is over, with the rise of free agency. Prior to 1975, players really weren't able to pick whom they played for, and after that time, they are. Many, many star players will now get to a point in their careers where a bidding war will ensue to bring them to a certain team, which often is the Yankees, incidentally, because they have a lot of money. . . .

[But] there are still players who are considered to be what are called "franchise players." They really embody the team, and you can't think of them in any other uniform. Now, Joe DiMaggio was that sort of player for the New York Yankees, a star player and symbolic of an era and an ethnic group. But I think that it's a mistake to romanticize that . . . because often those players stayed with the team simply because they had no other choice legally. Had they worked in the conditions post-1975, they might have done the same thing that many of the players post-1975 have done.

Romance is a great thing. Baseball is full of romantic notions, and many of them are true and not true at the same time. We can't possibly know if Joe DiMaggio would have switched to another team if he'd had the option, but since he didn't have the option, let's not give him too much credit for not having done that.

PV: And Joe DiMaggio was with the Yankees for sixteen years.

TW: We romanticize the notion of a player like DiMaggio staying with the Yankees and embodying the Yankees, and really perhaps what we're romanticizing is the era in which they played, and that era had as one if its conditions that the player wasn't really free to choose where he was going to work. Now labor historians . . . think of that as a great tragedy. If you're a shoe salesman, you're allowed to work for any company you want, but if you're a baseball player, up until 1975 you were technically owned by the team; your contract was owned. . . . So kids could grow up and be DiMaggio fans their whole lives . . . without worrying about him leaving, but when you look at the underpinnings of what created the system, [we see that] some good and some bad are there. . . .

PV: And you say that DiMaggio was a franchise player.

TW: Which is just a phrase applied by historians and the press. But a franchise player probably means two things: a player who is unequivocally identified with his team (or his franchise) and also a player upon whose work on the field the team can be built. . . .

PV: You mention the romanticizing of the franchise player's loyalty, and that reminds me that I began this research with the somewhat naive notion of these franchise players as basically good guys who pulled themselves up by their own bootstraps, who played hard for the same team for not that much money all their lives—like the man who worked for the factory for forty years and who would get a clock upon retirement. And then I assumed the current players were very flamboyant, displayed bad behavior, were sometimes associated with gambling—Pete Rose, for example. But then I read about John McGraw and Leo Durocher.

TW: [laughs.]

PV: What I read about Durocher was that he was twice very close to being indicted for gambling. So here comes the question. Are the players today really less moral, ethical, upstanding types, and are the players of the past really better men, morally speaking, or do we here, too, romanticize the past?

TW: There certainly is some romance at work. Players today and players throughout all of baseball history have been young men—often young men with an extraordinary talent which causes them to be treated differently in general by the public, often making more money than the average person, even in the [nineteen] twenties, thirties, forties; . . . they were often making six, seven, eight times what the electrician was making. And the temptations have always been indulged in by the players. The temptations are different to-day, and the milieu in which the people are working is different today. It's a national and sometimes an international media market that they work in.

And many, many players are good people who do not indulge in gambling or alcoholism or drugs or groupies. . . . And what has changed in addition to the milieu is that the media has changed. The media protected baseball players and other athletes and prob-ably celebrities from having their foibles exposed in public. There was an unwritten rule about that, and there was a cozy arrangement, unwritten but understood, by all involved that the role of the media was to help promote the sport of baseball or whatever entertain-ment medium was being written about, and the key moment of change also relates to the Yankees, which is such an important team in American culture. . . .

There was a book called *Ball Four* written by a player Jim Bouton that came out in the early seventies. . . . Bouton was a player who exposed candidly the behavior of other players on his team and on others. . . . (Quick aside: The New York Public Library in the year 1999 named Bouton's book one of the "One Hundred Most Im-portant Books of the Twentieth Century.") Baseball blackballed Bouton for many years, and it wasn't until only three or four years ago that he was finally invited back to Old Timers Day at Yankee Stadium. . . .

But before that, the sports autobiography . . . [was] about presenting a pretty picture for youth about a baseball hero, or for adults.

PV: And that does pretty well track with the changes in biography. Recently, it has been debunking; previously, biography was hagiography.

TW: Yeah, exactly.

PV: So that brings me to the next question. There's no question about the fact that Joe DiMaggio takes the function of a saint in this novella—

TW: Sure.

PV: And you see Santiago talking about DiMaggio the way, in another context, you would see him talking about a patron saint. . . . Who might Hemingway use today to provide that function in a novella?

TW: I have to go with my gut reaction. The guy who leaps into my mind is Cal Ripken Jr. [of the Baltimore Orioles], who played in 2,632 consecutive games throughout the 1980s and 1990s. He broke the hallowed record held by Lou Gehrig of 2,130 consecutive games, which most sportswriters and sports people and fans always considered unbreakable, and he did it playing through small broken bones and lots of muscle pulls . . .

He's also embodied a certain style of values. "Old school" is a phase that might be applied. He's a ballplayer's ballplayer: workmanlike, humble, ethical—all the things that we laud in a hero like DiMaggio. To my mind, . . . [these virtues] are truer of Ripken than of DiMaggio, especially with the recent biography [by Richard Ben Cramer] that shows him in a less than heroic light. And that's all part of the process of a new interpretation of DiMaggio. Hemingway probably knew it. . . .

PV: The problems of a Durocher, for example, would have been part of the working knowledge of anyone writing about him during the late forties and fifties; but in *The Old Man and the Sea*, Hemingway presented baseball players only in their best light for the fiction.

TW: Roger Kahn, in *The Boys of Summer* that came out in 1972, spoke here last year and answered the question "What changed? Why do we now have such interest in and knowledge of the foibles of these players?" He said that in the fifties, when he was writing about the Brooklyn Dodgers for the New York papers . . . there were things you just didn't consider writing about.

PV: This was the ethos of the time, in which Hemingway participated as well, that sports figures were presented in their best light. If we can turn to another topic now, that of the relationship between

Cuba and American baseball, could a Cuban person today be as interested in American major-league baseball?

TW: My answer is, definitely. . . . Some of our staff went to Cuba for the Baltimore Orioles' game against the Cuban National Team in '98 or '99, and our people couldn't get off the plane before they were besieged with questions about American major-league baseball. . . .

We think often of the thirties, forties, and fifties as a time when there was a golden age of kids playing baseball on sandlots in the United States, and baseball was kind of the only game for a while. It is still that way in these Latin America countries, and they know about the *gran ligas*, and when they get a chance to get baseball cards or a copy of baseball book, [these items] are very desirable. . . .

PV: So Castro hasn't prevented their access to American baseball?

TW: No. Castro loves baseball.

PV: Well, here's another question. Are there comparable Mike Gonzalezes or Dolf Luques today? Who are the players who have left Cuba and made it big in American baseball?

TW: . . . The leading one would be Orlando Hernandez, known as "El Duque." . . .

He's got the prototypical story. In fact, I believe there's a movie in production: He leaves Cuba on a raft or a boat and goes to Nicaragua rather than Florida. And here's where the modern era comes in. If he goes to Florida, he might be naturalized, and he would fit under the existing rules of major-league baseball—drafting. But in Nicaragua, he could remain a free agent. He's a smart guy and [has] some help from people. And [he's] one of a half dozen or maybe even a dozen people who have defected from the Cuban National Team over the last ten years. Goes to Nicaragua and eventually he signs with the Yankees, and within a year, he's pitching in the World Series.

Now, his brother Livan, actually his half brother, made it to the major leagues . . . and pitched in the World Series for the Florida Marlins and won a game or two and became a great hero during that time to Cuban people in Cuba, Cuban people in Florida, and fans in general. And the great story is that he has a brother who's even better! . . . Now, there are plenty of other players who've defected.

PV: But the big thing here is that these people had to defect. So their transition into American baseball had some political ramifications that were absent for Dolf Luque and Mike Gonzalez, who were free to move from one country to another. And, of course, absent from today's baseball scenario would be the Dick Sislers who went to Havana during the off-season.

TW: A lot of American Players still go to Latin America during the off-season to play.

PV: But not to Cuba.

TW: But not to Cuba.

PV: One of the things that Manolin and Santiago talk about as a topic within the topic of baseball is who the greatest manager was. Why is this an issue, and who would be named today?

TW: Ah!

PV: They talk about Dolf Luque and Durocher and McGraw. Many people at the time the novella was written would not have known who McGraw was. Who would [Santiago and Manolin] nominate today?

TW: Okay, the first half of the question—Why would being a manager be important?—is very hard to answer, actually; it's sort of an existential question. . . . The manager clearly calls all the shots on the team and sets the tone of how the game is going. . . . Baseball people pride themselves on understanding the game on strategic and a minutiae level, and the game to me is unlike any other game I know in that it is possible to have infinitesimally small advantages if you're a smart baseball manager. . . .

A discussion of the best managers in baseball today would include four of them: Tony La Russa of the St. Louis Cardinals; Joe Torre of the Yankees; Felipe Alou, recently deposed from the Expos; and Dusty Baker of the San Francisco Giants. . . . These are the guys that I zoom in on.

And what makes these people good managers is their understanding . . . of both the macro elements and the micro elements of the game. . . . All of these guys are ex-players, as most managers are, and these guys are thought of as . . . players' managers. They are not strict disciplinarians. They're not by any means hang-loose kind of guys, but they let the players play, and then they pull the strings. . . .

They tend not to exhibit a level of control over their players that, for example, Durocher and McGraw in another era were known for—curfews, dress codes, things like that. And maybe that's just a change in baseball generally or society generally or both.

It's interesting that La Russa and Torre are . . . white guys, both of Italian descent, and Felipe Alou is an Hispanic . . . and then Dusty Baker is an African American. . . . All of these guys have won the Manager of the Year award, but Alou and Baker have won it re-

peatedly. . . . Prior to about 1995, there was frequent pressure from
the press whenever a managerial opening would occur in baseball
to get the team to hire a minority, and both Alou and Baker would
qualify. Today we have thirty major-league baseball teams, and we
have eight or nine minority managers. . . . It's probably beginning
to be [proportionate] with the [number] of minority players.

It takes a special person to be a manager, it takes an intellect and
a leadership ability that many players don't have or don't develop.

These [La Russa, Torre, Alou, and Baker] are the guys that Hemingway would zoom in on. . . . Hemingway was a very good baseball
fan . . . and probably knew a lot about what it takes to manage a
baseball team. . . . At the time he was writing this book, there was
a perception about both African Americans and Hispanics in baseball that they were somehow junior partners in baseball, and Hemingway, living in Cuba, probably [understood] Cuban people
[better] in terms of their abilities. . . .

PV: I have one other area for discussion, and then we'll address anything you think we haven't touched. What about the diminishing
involvement of young people in baseball in the United States today,
. . . attributing the decline to the major-league baseball strike in
1994 and early '95 and that kids are now playing soccer, video
games—

TW: Using the Internet.

PV: Yeah. There's the idea that in the future, baseball will not be seen
as the dominant American sport. My questions to you are: (a) Do
you think this is true? And (b) Where would baseball in general fit
into the writing of *The Old Man and the Sea* at this point in time?
Would it be baseball or soccer?

TW: First of all, I do think it's true [that baseball is losing fans]. . . . This
is considered by many to be a big, big problem. Kids have many
sports to choose from—soccer, hockey, basketball, football . . .
[and] yes, American kids are not playing sandlot baseball like they
used to. . . .

But I think baseball in general will continue to grow. I heard Bud
Selig, the commissioner of baseball, talk in Milwaukee last week.
And he was asked about the Hispanic presence in the game. . . . And
it has grown and grown and grown, and the percentage of Latinos
is much greater today than ever before in major-league baseball.
And he said . . . it [the percentage of Latino players] will continue
to grow.

I think [baseball] is the purest example of the melting-pot concept that we have. You see Polish names, you see Italian names, you see Latino names, . . . you see African American people. . . . You see Jewish people, you see Asians now. I want to believe in the melting-pot concept in the United States, but I know that many sociologists and historians will give you evidence that it doesn't exist, that it's a noble ideal. But I think in a baseball clubhouse, as long as the guy can hit or pitch or whatever, it becomes kind of an ideal, almost utopian society. . . .

Would baseball be the sport that Hemingway . . . would use today . . . ? I still think it would. I think baseball has some peculiar characteristics . . . for whatever reason. . . . Fiction and nonfiction writers are drawn to baseball even today in far greater numbers than to football, basketball, hockey. And the way to prove this to yourself is to go into [a bookstore] and look for the baseball fiction, and . . . there will be at least ten times, if not thirty or forty times, as much fiction, poetry, essays written about baseball as there is [about other sports]. . . .

PV: But is there a short answer to the question, Would Hemingway still be using baseball today?

TW: Yes, I still think he would, and again, because it's the one sport that is accessible to writers and works for writers . . . but also it's now become, partly through Hemingway and a lot of other writers, the sport in America used to convey an idea of an America past. If you look at . . . baseball movies . . . in the 1980s, . . . we had *The Natural, Bull Durham, Field of Dreams, A League of Their Own*, which I believe was in the early nineties. All of these movies were big hits. . . . Two of those come from novels, *The Natural* and *Field of Dreams*. . . . Somehow, what I call a "literary sense" of America is conveyed in those pieces. . . .

Incidentally, *Eight Men Out* was also made in the eighties. . . . All of a sudden, you've got five great baseball movies in a very short time, . . . trying to look back to a perfect world that may or may not have existed. Baseball, rightly or wrongly, is used by a lot of conservatives as a story about America's golden past. . . .

PV: Your comment is really applicable to *The Old Man and the Sea*. Every aspect of baseball in that novella is to contribute the feeling of a perfect world—a time, a space, a character, a setting where things are done right, where things are perfected—

TW: And simple, as well, as a result.

PV: There's not the complexity, there's not the ambiguity that's so complicating in the present. . . .

TW: I totally agree, and I love the book for those reasons. Not that I want to have a world that is that simple, but it's nice to think about one. . . . And then you'll get back on the interstate—

PV: Or the Internet . . .

TW: And you'll have a complex, fragmented, difficult world. I think that's one of the functions, one of the reasons that baseball is used by writers of today—to evoke a simplicity and an uncomplicated sense.

PV: I want to express my gratitude because you've opened so many interesting doors.

TOPICS FOR ORAL OR WRITTEN EXPLORATION

1. Rewrite the dialogue between Manolin and Santiago on pages 17 though 23 of *The Old Man and the Sea* and situate their comments in the modern-day baseball world. Using information from the interview with Tim Wiles, make this dialogue as specific as possible.

2. Identify a sport that is popular among your friends, such as football or basketball, and respond to one of the following:

   • Rewrite the dialogue on pages 17 through 23 of the novella using heroes from that sport.

   • Write an essay in which you identify and analyze the values implied by the sport that you have chosen. (For example, football is associated with great speed, physical power, and violent contact.) Explain fully the values associated with this sport and how these values would impact the theme of the novella.

3. *The Old Man and the Sea* might be the title of a novella describing Anselmo Hernandez's escape from Cuba. Write a short story in which you imagine the experiences of Hernandez at sea. Use information derived from the novella about marine organisms and climate to build the setting; use the specifics of Santiago's characterization to fill out Hernandez's description. Then consider the plot: Could it continue to revolve around the conflict between man versus nature or man versus himself? Would the conflict have to shift to that of man versus man? What would the climax and denouement of your short story be if Anselmo Hernandez is your protagonist? Finally, consider the theme of your short story: What would you want the reader to understand as its main idea?

4. Remove all religious references from the novella and decide with what these references might be replaced. Look at pages 64 and 65 specifically as you think through your response. What or whom might Santiago invoke to obtain a favor or goal? How would the character of Santiago be changed if he made no references to religion? Would the deletion of religion create a thematic change in the novella?

5. In different places in this chapter, mention is made of people who have come to the United States from Cuba: Anselmo Hernandez, Elian Gonzalez, Orlando Hernandez. Write an essay in which you compare and contrast their reasons for arriving in the United States. Should U.S. immigration law give preference to one person over another who leaves Cuba for the United States?

6. Anselmo Hernandez and Elian Gonzalez risked their lives at sea; so did Santiago. Write a journal entry in which you express your judg-

ment about the value of the risks these persons took in relation to the goals they were seeking.

7. Bad sportsmanship seems to characterize athletics today as much as does good sportsmanship. Write a letter to a younger person in which you extol the virtues of being a good sport. You might recall having observed someone or a team demonstrate poor sportsmanship; contrast this behavior with examples of the characters and sports figures from *The Old Man and the Sea*, as well as with baseball players identified in the interview with Tim Wiles.

8. Tim Wiles states that baseball represents the true "melting pot" in the United States. Write an argument about sports as an equalizing force in American society using one of the following prompts:

   • Baseball as the great example of the melting pot in American society
   • A sport played at your school that brings all racial, socioeconomic, and gender groups in the school population together.

   You may also wish to argue the opposite position on one of the above topics.

9. Baseball, Mom, and apple pie: These words represent clichés of the American experience. Freewrite in your journal about the truth of that statement. Do each of these entities represent America to you? If not, what are three things you would put forth that represent America?

SUGGESTED READINGS AND WORKS CITED

Abel, David. "Night Fishing in Havana Takes Patience—And a Long Line." *Christian Science Monitor* 90:133 (5 June 1998): 7.

Aguilar Eloy O. "Religion Grows in Cuba." AP NY-08–16–97. Free Cuba Foundation. At: www.fiu.edu/~fcf/churchgrows81897.html; accessed 27 August 2001.

Bouton, Jim. *Ball Four: My Life and Hard Times Throwing the Knuckleball in the Big Leagues*. Ed. Leonard Shecter. New York: Dell Publishing, 1970.

Bruni, Frank. "Bush Administration Showing Willingness to Enforce Law on Visiting Cuba." *New York Times*, 5 August 2001, 5:9.

Burros, Marian. "Havana's Not for Eating, but Eating Can Be Fun." *New York Times*, 5 August 2001, 5:8, 20.

Centano, Miguel Angel. *Toward a New Cuba? Legacies of a Revolution*. Boulder, CO: Lynne Rienner Publishers, 1997.

Chaffee, Wilber A., Jr., and Gary Prevost, eds. *Cuba: A Different America*. Totowa, NJ: Rowman & Littlefield, 1992.

"Denial of Food and Medicine: The Impact of the U.S. Embargo on the Health and Nutrition in Cuba." The American Association for World Health Report, Summary of Findings, March 1997. At www.cubasolidarity.net/aawh.html; accessed 23 December 2001.

"Dreams Lead All the Way to Havana." *New York Times*, 12 June 2001, B:1.

Fainaru, Steve, and Ray Sanchez. *The Duke of Havana: Baseball, Communism, and the Search for the American Dream*. New York: Villard Books, 2001.

Fuertes, Norberto. *Ernest Hemingway Rediscovered*. New York: Charles Scribner's Sons, 1988.

Hostetter, Martha, ed. *Cuba*. New York: H. W. Wilson, 2001.

Kahn, Roger. *The Boys of Summer*. Evanston, IL: Holtzman Press, 1972.

Kirk, John M. *Between God and the Party: Religion and Politics in Revolutionary Cuba*. Tampa: University of South Florida Press, 1989.

Linger, Eloise, et al. *Cuban Transitions at the Millennium*. Largo, MD: International Development Options, 2000.

Reynolds, Michael. *Hemingway: The Final Years*. New York: W. W. Norton, 1999.

"The U.S. Embargo and Health Care in Cuba: Myth Versus Reality." U.S. Department of State. At http://secretary.state.gov/www/briefings/statements/970514.html; accessed 23 December 2001.

"What Ails Cuba's Health Service?" *Economist* 349: 8094 (14 November 1998): 40.

Zimbalist, Andrew S. *The Cuban Economy: Measurement and Analysis of Socialist Performance*. Baltimore: Johns Hopkins University Press, 1989.

Index

About the Author

PATRICIA DUNLAVY VALENTI is Professor in the Department of English, Theatre, and Languages at the University of North Carolina, Pembroke. She is also coordinator of the Graduate Program in English Education there. Her primary area of scholarship is American literature. Among her publications is *To Myself a Stranger: A Biography of Rose Hawthorne Lathrop* (1991).